ADVANCED MEDIATION ADVOCACY
From Contest to Collaboration

Each human being is unique, as is each society. It follows logically then, that no two conflicts are the same. Much as we would like it, there is no magic formula that, once discovered, can be used to end all conflicts. But there are certain principles arising out of my experience in Northern Ireland that I believe are universal. First, I believe there is no such thing as a conflict that can't be ended. They are created and sustained by human beings. They can be ended by human beings, no matter how ancient the conflict, no matter how hateful or how hurtful, peace can prevail.

U.S. Senator George Mitchell
Principles of Peace, BBC Richard Dimbleby Lecture, 1998;
Investiture of the Liberty Medal July 4, 1998

You need to suspend your reaction when you feel like striking back, to listen when you feel like talking back, to ask questions when you feel like telling your opponent the answers, to bridge your differences when you feel like pushing for your way, and to educate when you feel like escalating. Breakthrough.

William Ury
Getting Past No – Negotiating in Difficult Situations 1991

To Michel Kallipetis KC

Friend, colleague, mentor, guide and mediator of choice

We may not agree on everything, but everything we do agree on gives me comfort and confidence in our general direction of travel.

Thank you.

ADVANCED MEDIATION ADVOCACY
From Contest to Collaboration

A PERSONAL VIEW

ANDREW GOODMAN

LLB MBA PhD FCIArb FInstCPD FRSA Barrister
CEDR Mediator and IMI Mediation Advocate

Professor of Conflict Management and Dispute Resolution Studies, Rushmore University

Convenor, Standing Conference of Mediation Advocates

Director, College of Mediators

Director, Association of Mediation Assessors, Trainers and Instructors

Distinguished Fellow, International Academy of Mediators

Of the Inner Temple, a Master of the Bench

MEDIATION PUBLISHING

Disclaimer

This work is not intended to be comprehensive. It is not a substitute for appropriate legal advice. Neither the author not the publisher accept any responsibility for loss occasioned to any person acting or refraining from acting as a result of material contained in this publication.

ISBN 978-1-85811-727-0
Ebook ISBN 978-1-85811-505-4
Printed and Designed in the UK

Mediation Publishing,
Suite 74, 17 Holywell Hill
St Albans
AL1 1DT, UK

www.mediationpublishing.com

Foreword

By the Rt Hon. Baroness Carr of Walton-on-the Hill, Lady Chief Justice of England and Wales

I am delighted to welcome Andrew Goodman's latest contribution to the expanding literature on mediation. As a companion to his work, *Effective Mediation Advocacy*, Andrew continues to promote the idea that practitioners should have specialist knowledge of representing parties at mediation, that the endeavour is intellectually challenging and rewarding, and that it is very different from trial advocacy and should certainly be taken seriously.

It is at an opportune moment in the development of mediation in this jurisdiction that this book arrives. The Court of Appeal in *Churchill* v *Merthyr Tydfil County Borough Council* [2023] EWCA Civ 1416 held that *Halsey* v *Milton Keynes General NHS Trust* [2004] EWCA Civ 576 did not prevent courts from mandating that parties engage in alternative dispute resolution. Parties should be mindful of the shift in approach to a system that, as Andrew describes it, gives advocates 'freedom to be creative and promote cohesion between the parties' interests rather than maintain division.'

In this volume Andrew takes a number of disparate topics and offers an individual analysis delivered in such a way as to provoke new thought, alongside practical tools for advocates engaging in mediation. He starts with the premise that mediation is essentially a collaborative process: any successful outcome must be based on consensus, necessarily resulting from a creative approach by all those involved, to a greater or lesser extent. Ironically, what drives the parties into that process is usually conflict, which forces them initially to take at least a competitive if not a combative stance, entirely reflective of what advocates are trained to do. Usually, they enter the process from a contest over their client's rights.

How then does the advocate move from contest to collaboration? Andrew makes the case that there is a course of transition – a dynamic change in professional representation during the mediation procedure, leading ultimately to creative options for mutual gain. Along the way he looks at evaluative mediation, appellate mediation schemes, the move to online work, and the ethical dilemmas that spring up when least expected.

But it is in particular in his departure from this jurisdiction to offer advice on the international work of a mediation advocate, dealing with cross-border and multi-jurisdictional problems, that Andrew brings his wealth of experience to his readership. We are only now catching up with the advances made in India, Turkey, Singapore and the many other jurisdictions with which he is familiar, as mediator, trainer, educator and advocate.

I hope that, like its companion volume, this book will find its way to law libraries and practitioners' bookshelves from Kathmandu to Goa, Prague to Cape Town, and Hong Kong to Dublin. I am very pleased to commend it.

The Rt Hon. The Baroness Carr of Walton-on-the-Hill

The Lady Chief Justice of England and Wales

May 2024

Preface

On 30 October, 2020 the International Academy of Mediators in conjunction with the Hong Kong Mediation Centre hosted a symposium on international commercial mediation in Asia. One of the components was an interactive panel discussion hosted by C W Ling with Prof. Dwight Golann, Michel Kallipetis KC and Jody Sin entitled 'Manipulative Advocates: How to Respond'. The fact that mediators felt it necessary to hold such a discussion suggests that mediation advocacy is finally coming of age. At last it is being taken seriously by both mediators and advocates. And, at the time of writing, the International Mediation Institute is revising its mediation advocacy competency criteria, and training courses are being delivered on a regular basis internationally in India, Turkey, Hong Kong, Brunei and Singapore, as well as the United Kingdom, and as part of the recognition of core competencies in cross-border and cross-cultural work.

In October, 2022, in delivering his contribution to training in mediation advocacy for the Hong Kong Bar Association, Kallipetis KC said "Mediation advocacy is the advocacy of the future. Those who embrace it will be remembered. Those who do not will be forgotten." This work presumes he is entirely correct (as he usually is), and the field is now expanding to include regular online debate concerning professional practice, procedure and ethical issues in a wide range of jurisdictions with generically consistent discussion.

Advanced Mediation Advocacy is designed to follow and complement its companion title *Effective Mediation Advoca*cy,[1] which has been published since 2005 in various editions and imprints in the United Kingdom, India, Hong Kong, Nigeria and Turkey (including the Turkish language), both for practitioners and students. This new volume is intended to give a framework and linguistic structure to what many practitioners have been doing intuitively. It will hopefully provide highly pragmatic advice in distinct sections - developing the role of the mediation advocate in specific tasks; dealing with common problems, including some fairly common ethical dilemmas faced by practitioners; preparing a more sophisticated negotiation strategy by building and defending ATNAs, and participating fully in option generation; understanding the nuancing of advocacy in evaluative mediation, and its consequences for Courts of Appeal mediation schemes; getting the best out of online mediation, to which most of us have migrated at least in part as a result of Covid 19; and planning for and engaging in cross-border, cross-cultural or multi-party international mediation, a subject given the added dimension of enforceability due to ratification in 2020 by sufficient states of the United Nations Convention on International Settlement Agreements Resulting from Mediation ("the Singapore Convention") 2019, and the United Kingdom becoming a signatory in May, 2023.

---

1 4th edition 2024 (Mediation Publishing)

Following on from my earlier work I am keen to examine the true nature of mediation advocacy – coping with and reacting to change throughout the process; managing the client, but also and perhaps more controversially, managing the mediator. And adding real value in helping your client arrive at the best available settlement as you engage with a collaborative process that will change your outlook and transform your approach to dealing with disputes, and potentially, to dealing with people generally.

In particular I am interested in discussing the dynamic movement from a party representative being defensive of his or her client's position to becoming visionary in respect of that same client's interests. How do you move from contentious to collaborative, from combative or competitive, to creative? After considering this theme I will look at the role of the advocate in building and defending the client's ATNAS to include seeking out and marshalling relevant information, applying and valuing it, and considering the impact of change during a dynamic process. Then we shall consider some common ethical problems that face counsel, which point up questions as to the true nature of the relationship between mediator, counsel and client, and professional or contractual rules impacting on conduct.

The market for mediation services in many jurisdictions demands a more evaluative approach from the mediator, often bordering on, and sometimes filling the gaps between mediation, conciliation and early neutral evaluation. How should the professional advocate deal with that, other than by falling back on the orthodoxy of traditional practice? This is a subject ripe for discussion, and I start by scratching the surface with what I think are obvious propositions.

I believe this obviously leads to analysing the advocate's role in dealing with Court of Appeal annexed mediation schemes where one party has already obtained the judgment of the court below. What is the impact of court findings, and what can be done to move the parties away from this fixed power imbalance?

Next, I would like to move first into the international arena to look at both cross-border and cross-cultural work and its implications for mediator selection, client and advocate preparation, cross-border or inter-cultural ethical considerations, and second at the implications of the Singapore Convention; and finally, at the migration to online work which may enable practitioners to engage in more international work at a much lower cost than might previously have been the case.

Some of the content may be familiar to audiences in Singapore, Bangkok, Lagos, New Delhi, Hong Kong, Prague, Ankara, Istanbul and Cape Town since many of the ideas that I advance in this book were first prepared for and presented at various mediation conferences, and to delegates at mediation advocacy skills training programmes that were given by me at these cities variously between 2017 and 2020, before lockdown, and since. It is a personal view, born out of some 30 years mediation practice and consultancy in approaching 20 different jurisdictions, and 45 years as an independent professional advocate. It is designed to provoke thought, stimulate debate and, as much as it can, normalise mediation in the minds of legal and other professional practitioners. By the same token I try to keep my views as generic as possible, burdened as I am with the baggage of my own jurisdiction, where civil justice is dominated by expensive one-way costs shifting for the winner, and while the expense is real, the costs-shifting can be very much a chimera due to the irrecoverable costs element.

We have suffered since March, 2020 and continue to be affected by a period of significant change due to the pandemic, and need to prepare for further potential disruption. One of the facets of that change, and our response to it, has been the ability of the mediation world – as many other service industries - to meet the challenge of moving online for meetings, negotiation, full scale mediation, and for training, and to dispense with face-to-face work, although the latter is gradually returning, and certain clients both prefer and are prepared to wait for that service. Even if online work is now sustainable as future normality, many more practitioners prefer the close, face-to-face practice which has been the hallmark of exercising skills in addressing the breakdown and subsequent reintegration of inter-personal or business relationships.

Over the period of writing this book there have been new mediation or conciliation acts in India and Nigeria, and at last the courts of England and Wales appear to be ready to grasp the nettle of compulsion in having parties engage in mediation. At least we have moved from the suggestive to, in certain circumstances, the directive,[2] and as a result of that freedom, as I write moves are afoot to amend the relevant Civil Procedure Rules in England and Wales.[3]

I also wish to both thank Dame Sue Carr for her kind contribution of a foreword and pay tribute to her extraordinary talent as she embarks upon the historic challenge of becoming the first female Chief Justice in British history. I am grateful for her time, her advice and wisdom, and the support she has always offered the SCMA as patron and the wider mediation community.

I have tried to offer advice encompassing both face-to-face and digital methods of working in this book, the contents of which must, of course, be regarded as a snapshot in time. I do hope though, that it offers value to the reader well into the future before, like most of us, we are overtaken by AI.

Andrew Goodman

Chancery Lane, London

May, 2024.

---

2 See *Churchill v Merthyr Tydfil County Borough Council* [2023] EWCA Civ 1416

3 CPR 3.1(2)(o), 28.7.(1)(d), 29.2(1A),44.5(e)

Contents

Table of Cases

Table of Conventions, Rules and Statutes

Introduction: Transition in Mediation Advocacy

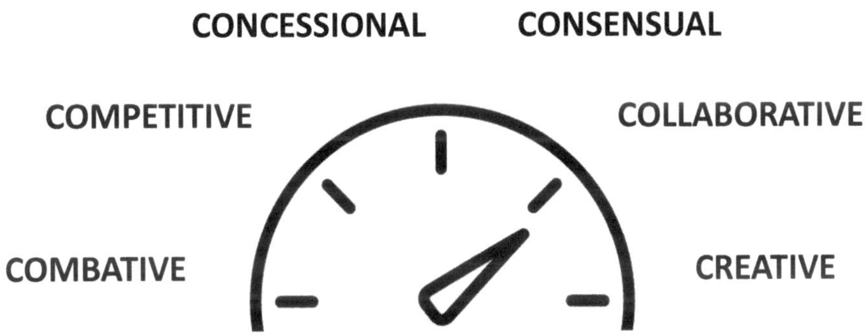

Dynamic change in professional representation during the mediation process

Mediation advocacy is founded on two principles which practitioners would do well to remember.

First, we are focusing on what is important to the client - not to the Court and not to the law. This requires the discovery of and a familiarity with the client's business, financial, personal or social affairs to an extent that goes well beyond what we would need to prosecute or defend a legal cause of action, and which drives the client's expectations and emotions. It also challenges the advocate's training, experience and orthodoxy.

Second, mediation, unlike most civil justice processes, is not a vehicle for deciding who is right in the dispute. The mediator is unlikely to care who is right, unless to do so has a significant impact on advancing a settlement which is durable. And if the client is trying to use the process simply to demonstrate he is right, as a precursor to an open court vindication, he is unlikely to get a settlement at all. Mediation, rather, is a medium by which the client can become better off in terms of outcome than he would be without it, though curiously, by accepting that the other participants in the dispute also need to feel 'better off'. The advocate needs to focus on what might potentially be available – including things far beyond the remit of the Court – that both parties may find acceptable as an outcome, rather than just his or her own client.

In this discussion I want to explore these two simple propositions to examine how they change us from being trial advocates to mediation advocates, and in so doing to recognise that a different mindset is required to represent parties at mediation. If that is right, it will follow that different preparation, a different approach to the process, a different expectation, and a different way of valuing available outcomes will all be necessary for the practitioner.

Mediation then, is essentially a collaborative process since any successful outcome must be based on consensus, necessarily resulting from a creative approach by all those involved, to a greater or lesser extent. Yet ironically, what drives the parties into that process is usually conflict, which forces them initially to take at least a competitive if not a combative stance, entirely reflective of what advocates are trained to do. Usually they enter the process from a contest.

That is because most disputes are dominated by a rights-based evaluation of the parties' respective positions, either themselves or by their lawyers, as a matter of legal construct. The Rule of Law is a rights-based system which ultimately derives from the social contract between the state and its citizens. It is dependent on social compliance with rules affecting civil liberties – of course, now more than ever – in exchange for personal, civil, contractual, and property rights which the state will protect and enforce on the application of the citizen to the civil justice system when those rights have been or are about to be interfered with. The state as guarantor of citizens' rights invests itself with an interest in the management of the dispute, if not the outcome, instituting a framework of rituals and measures to try and ensure necessary fairness. The state also runs the justice system as a business (however poorly managed), deriving fees from litigants and taxes from advocates and employees, and even being incorporated into the UK's invisible earnings for its economy and balance of payments.

The modern state-managed dispute resolution process is entirely a rule-based universe populated by substantive and procedural law and practised by its exponents – the lawyers – who are trained in risk management to evaluate likely outcomes measured against a cost/benefit analysis. It is particularly so in an expensive jurisdiction with a one-way costs shifting regime, where the loser pays the legal costs of the winner, subject to an assessment of proportionality and reasonableness by the Court. It could be said that in the jurisdiction of England and Wales modern litigation outcomes are all about risk management. In the United States a cynic would say litigation is simply part of the cost of doing business.

As I explained in *Effective Mediation Advocacy*,[1] ADR systems are based on the recognition and investigation of the interests of participants and are not confined to merely examining the legal rights of the parties. Such an investigation gives rise to both aspiration – a hopeful outcome – and a sense of balance, since the process demands an outcome which ultimately is acceptable to both sides, not merely one. There is an overlap between the delivery of civil justice and ADR because the first must and the second tends to start by operating in the shadow of the law. But there is no true correlation, and there is little point in categorising mediation as an outlier of the justice system, particularly since courts in many jurisdictions are looking at making mediation a compulsory precursor to entry into litigation.

At the time of writing, what the Ministry of Justice has billed as 'compulsory mediation' is again under review. We may end up with a multi-door entry system for access to civil justice in which administrative officers of the Court decide on issue by suitability whether a claim should be mediated, arbitrated as non-binding early evaluation or litigated, as works well in Nigeria. 'Small claims' will be directed to mediation as a matter of course.

Yet mediation is presently independent of the civil justice system save for those areas where the Court wishes to exercise a supervisory jurisdiction, or the Court recognises the convenience of outsourcing its caseload when safe and appropriate to do so, or when parties require the machinery of the state operating through the court process to enforce a settlement born out of mediation where one party has failed to honour his or her bargain to the other.

But this is less about the process, and more about the actors engaged in it on a professional basis, since it concerns the development of specialist professional skills, and I proceed on the basis that you are familiar with the concepts that sit behind mediation; that you have attended in some capacity or another at least one or more mediations and you are sufficiently familiar with its procedural nature in one of its primary forms.

The reader of *Effective Mediation Advocacy* will know I take the view that mediation advocacy, irrespective of how you define it, or what you think it amounts to, requires specialist skill and specialist knowledge, not the least of which is knowledge of the process and procedure. But beyond that, for most lawyers it is an adjunct of what they do as part of their ordinary practice. Lawyers and professional advocates come to represent parties at mediation through the prism of their orthodox training which makes them engage with their client's affairs by first analysing their client's position in the context of what the law requires of them, and what evidence they will need to triumph in the contest which is litigation. Conventional litigators may never get beyond that.

Those who are experienced in mediation, who have a more sophisticated – even enlightened – view and have been proactive in developing their mediation advocacy skills, will at least add value to their practice. They look for options for mutual gain, sufficient to provide longer term, more flexible, more innovative, more commercial, more cohesive, and also more durable

1 4th Edition, 2024 London, Mediation Publishing.

outcomes with which to satisfy their client. Potentially this represents a big win for the lawyer in terms of the client relationship, which will become more intense, and lawyer reputation for both modernity of approach and helping to deliver something the client truly needs.

Often these 'options for mutual gain' – I suppose we could say OMG – are to be found in extra-legal solutions. It may be that they can only be found there, depending upon the circumstances. Perhaps that is why the journey from conventional litigator to innovative and creative problem solver is hard for so many. In my view that outing involves a change of mind set which takes the lawyer through five distinct stances, from combative through competitive to consensual, thence to collaborative and from there to creative.

I approach these ideas optimistically. For the last 80 years or so, as a class, lawyers have managed to reinvent themselves for their commercial benefit, occasionally for the survival of their practice. Lawyers are nothing if not adaptable. Whenever their workload was threatened, they would find a nice and interesting area of burgeoning commercial activity and embrace it, capture it as an area of professional occupation by having the courts or legislature regulate it, and then by making themselves indispensable in interpreting the regulation by prosecuting and defending supposed breaches, come to monopolise it.

A good example is arbitration, known in ancient Greek, early Chinese and Biblical times as a system of private dispute resolution. In England from its inception in pre-recorded history through four chronological periods,[2] Anglo-Saxon, Medieval, 16th to 18th Century, and Modern, lawyers variously played little part until the whole regimen was captured by statutory enactment. The trades run by medieval guilds resolved disputes by the parties themselves arguing in front of a master or senior member of the guild or trades association in a process that was legalistic neither in form nor language. Increasingly throughout the nineteenth century access to the courts was required by parties to enforce arbitral awards, with the consequent engagement of lawyers. After another hundred years or so, arbitration had become so legalistic, time consuming and inordinately expensive that the Arbitration Act 1996 was enacted to remind everyone engaged of the primacy of the parties in the management of the process.[3]

It is hard to tell whether the creeping juridification of mediation will push it in the same direction as arbitration, so that mediation simply becomes a by-product of the inefficiency, tardiness, expense and inflexibility of the courts, but regulated by the civil justice system and operated exclusively by lawyers, rather than a truly alternative method of dispute resolution. The most recent direction of travel in the UK suggests the word 'alternative' will shortly be removed, to be replaced with something more complementary: 'negotiated'. We are already seeing this in Italy, Turkey, Greece and India due

2 Arbitration procedure in England: past, present and future. J. Martin, H. Hunter. Arbitration International, Volume 1, Issue 1, 1 April 1985.
3 On 25 May 2024 the proposed new Arbitration Bill then passing through the House of Lords review stage was lost when Parliament was prorogued for the July 2024 election.

to the monopolistic interests (and, certainly, intentions) of lawyers and their relationship with governing political parties, if not Government. So much for the inventiveness of lawyers!

Tilting at Windmills

Arguably the civil justice system – now exposed as such by the consequences of Covid 19 – is really on its knees, and the move towards online courts or even the use of artificial intelligence will not disguise the growing gap between the supposed delivery of justice and what citizens are actually provided with by the state. If you had to design a brand-new justice system you would not start from where we are now – reminiscent of the old joke about the American tourists lost deep in the Irish countryside, seeking directions from a local. It probably needs a completely new approach. Why do I say that having been a practitioner for over 40 years?

All binary justice systems are designed to create a winner and a loser. That is a very straightforward idea in criminal law where the choice is between a finding of guilt or innocence (dispensing for the moment with a process that requires the burden of proof to be allocated between the parties). In civil law the complainant will seek to establish that the respondent has broken or interfered with a right owned by or duty owed to him by the respondent and prove the legally enforceable consequences flowing from such an act or omission. But as between the parties, the process is also designed to create a loser. Statistically that means from the outset by way of design 50% of the parties to a trial will be dissatisfied with the outcome and wish they had never entered the process.

However, in real terms, 50% is the minimum. When you take into account the cost – particularly irrecoverable cost – the loss of management time, opportunity cost, damage to reputation, damage to relationships, the stress engendered by the experience and the potential lasting psychological damage of coming under intense scrutiny as a witness, and being pronounced upon by a judge, many winners also wish they had never entered into the process, even if they initiated it. Conservatively let us say then that a figure substantially more than 50% of the participants in any binary civil justice system wish afterwards, or some time before that, they had not been involved.

Now let us suppose that you run a business and produce a single product. You know that more than 50% of your customers are dissatisfied with that product. That being the case, how long will you stay in business? The allegory is obvious.

If you hold a state monopoly on civil enforcement, that question does not arise, no matter how costly, how slow, how under-resourced, undercapitalised, under-staffed .... and I could go on, but I think you have the point. In terms of design, would a modern civil justice system base itself entirely on a binary process?

As I have said, and experienced, in Nigeria, the Multi-door Court System makes mediation and other forms of what we call ADR, such as early neutral evaluation, an integral part of the civil justice process from the outset at issue. A registrar will assign cases to a particular track at entry level, and in so doing decide at the earliest of party engagement with the court whether a binary approach is the optimum choice for that case. The same can be said of the High Court in Nepal, which has 85 district registries with mediation offices performing the same function.

It is well to remember that the delivery of justice by the state is a mark of civilised society, of which a fair, accessible and open justice system is a fundamental part. To marginalise large sections of the population by making access to justice unaffordable by pursuing a policy of making civil justice cost neutral to the state is more the mark of an authoritarian regime. As also is the centralising of courts at the expense of local justice, by shutting down court buildings; and the obscuring of judicial decision making from public view by putting it online, using cost as an excuse.

Temporarily at the time of writing the crisis in court management brought about by Covid is reversing that trend. Some of the 83 apparently redundant buildings on the court estate which had either been sold off or mothballed as a result of the Ministry of Justice's internal review in 2016 are now needed again, as a response to significant delays in the system. In addition, 'pop-up' courts may become a familiar sight as we gradually come back to face-to-face hearings.

So, whether for the good reasons that the mediation industry promotes, or the bad reasons that our civil justice system suppresses, mediation for those in the know, has got to be part of modern practice, whether working as a contentious or transactional lawyer, an advocate, an insurance claims manager or loss adjuster, a construction industry professional, an estate or other property manager, or a forensic or private client accountant. And it is to those whom this is addressed. They will have a head start over traditionalists who do not want to normalise mediation and will avoid it even if required to engage in it by the court rules.

The Transition

My two most sage pieces of advice to the mediation advocate are simple. Since mediation is merely a tool upon which to focus, and with which to try to obtain what your client really needs, by learning what is important to him, rather than you, it should be used whenever appropriate to do so.

First, do not intellectualise mediation, just engage with it as a normal extension to your practice. Like any good artisan you must know how to use the correct tool at your disposal, properly and with skill.

Second, do whatever it takes as a professional to get the best available outcome for your client from the process. If that means devising a strategy which requires you to change your style as a lawyer, your manner, your outlook, or your normal approach to a piece of work, so be it. You will have to adapt from using a dispute resolution system which is divisive and competitive, to one that gives you the freedom to be creative and promote cohesion between the parties' interests rather than maintain division, even if you feel the need to protect your client's more narrow, legal case by using 'without prejudice' nomenclature. You will have to assuage your winning mentality by transitioning to an acceptance that both parties need a satisfactory outcome, in other words, both need to 'win', and you have to participate in bringing that about.

Making this adjustment is not easy, and for the professional advocate there will always be a residual desire founded on the competitive, even combative instinct that is generally present at the commencement of any piece of contentious work and is almost certainly present in any dispute that arrives at mediation only after it has already become litigious.

The word advocate is derived from the Latin, *ad vocare*, literally meaning to call across, summon, call in aid to you, or to your side, or party. For a number of years before the expression 'mediation advocacy' was accepted into wider use, and adopted by the International Mediation Institute in 2012, its detractors argued there was no place for advocacy in mediation, because its fundamental nature was consensual, and the expression was an oxymoron. As more lawyers in more jurisdictions became engaged in representing clients at mediation, they did so on the back of litigating the same dispute and related the phrase to what they were doing.[4] Only afterwards, with a more mature appreciation of the subtlety with which they could achieve a better outcome for their clients, did some practitioners come to understand that mediation advocacy requires a more sophisticated, and more nuanced approach calling for a very different mindset from the traditional model they had been taught and used, and an appreciation of what is really a very different function.

How, then, does the advocate change his or her mindset to get the best out of mediation?

I often hear it said that younger lawyers are much more aggressive in their trial work these days. I am not sure whether that is true, or a product of a changing court process, a response to client expectation, or simply my ageing. Aggression is, perhaps unfortunately, one way in which lawyers demonstrate they are earning their money and supposedly doing their best for their clients. When I was in full time practise at the Bar apparently – and I didn't know at the time – I was regarded as a very aggressive advocate. I would not then have regarded that as a bad thing, rather quite a compliment. I was doing what I thought was best for my clients by running my cases in a reasonably confrontational way because I felt I was being paid to be my client's champion or my client's hired gun.

For most people when they go to a solicitor to sort out their problems, they actually want somebody to stand up and act as their champion, partly because they're not capable of doing it themselves, and partly because the legal system is devised to require sound, qualified and experienced representation, and partly because the media gives rise to that expectation.

4 At the time of writing, the Bar Standard Board's Professional Statement summarises a barrister's characteristics (at page 24) and its Curriculum and Asssessment Strategy which sets out its prescribed advocacy assessment criteria (at page 26). These both appear to confine 'advocacy' to the classic court setting and appear entirely ignorant of non-Court Based Dispute Resolutiom. That attitude must soon change.

The mediation process asks advocates to do something which is different to that. But the civil justice system, as any binary system, must result in confrontation. That, as I have said, is necessarily the starting position, and a client will already think his or her lawyer has to be robust because offering to settle is apparently a sign of weakness.

The collaborative lawyer in contentious work is still a rare species, although such a notion has steadily been gaining adherents in the practice of family disputes. Not only are these relationship-driven, but they are also often concerned with the welfare of children, and outcomes generally have to factor in the future, if any, of such relationships and how they are going to be conducted. The context can give rise to an atmosphere which can be highly charged and emotional. But collaborative lawyers have also discovered that it is less costly for the client than a confrontational approach and leads to better outcomes. It is also much easier to mediate if a third-party neutral is needed to manage negotiation, particularly where there is a need to absorb reactive devaluation by a client's lawyers who assume, and are wary of, bias in dealings coming from the other side. But in more general civil litigation, such strong emotional drivers are either absent or, if there, tend to sit below the surface and the participants either cannot see them or will deliberately suppress them.

The issue immediately at hand is the interference with your client's rights and what remedy the court will provide. A confrontational or at least competitive approach to winning the case is usually necessary, even if only to jockey the parties into settlement negotiations from a position of perceived strength and then drive them forward on your terms, because the advocate has been taught that is what success looks and feels like, and that it is his or her achievement.

What do I mean by confrontational? It can be little more than forcefully setting out your arguments and saying why the other side has less prospect of winning their case at trial that does your client. Does that not reflect how many mediation advocates prepare their written position statement and contextualise their opening remarks at the first plenary session? Is that something of which to disapprove? For parties to a commercial dispute, it may be necessary to have such an analysis presented by their lawyer. However toxic that may be to the atmosphere the mediator is trying to create, this may simply be the appropriate place to start, subject only to the caveat that making a generalisation about this is probably not helpful. But it may simply be the necessary groundwork which enables the client to give vent to his anger, frustration, upset or other emotion, something simply not available to him in court.

If the factual matrix of any particular mediation centres on party 'rights' and remains focused on issues dealing with such rights, and so develops into a managed negotiation which confines the discussion between the participants to the future maintenance of, dealing with, addition to, or exchange of such rights, the lawyer may not wish to move away from confrontation mode because he sees the process as a vehicle to negotiate competitively. He may well see the desired outcome as a potential 'win' for his or her client, and mediation purists will find this uncomfortable. Yet, in this context, surely there is a place for tactics and strategy when representing clients in mediation. For the lawyer it compares favourably with what he would normally be called upon to do in litigation. It is a cosmetic change of forum, and venue, and the principal actor simply changes from being a judge to a mediator. But otherwise, there is very little adjustment.

I think many of my mediator colleagues would be disappointed with that analysis.

To get the best out of the mediation process the parties' lawyers need to understand the possibilities now open to their clients. That may require more time and more effort on their part, but the benefit to their practice of having a truly happy client is well worth considering, and the factual matrix presenting itself in the dispute may often not anyway fit the mould of a rights-based approach. Contrary to my previous scenario, which offers comfort to the kind of lawyer who has no desire to change his or her approach to a claim moving across from litigation, mediation advocates should always look beyond the rights-based approach, to help the client investigate the added value in such possibilities. Added value should always be available in mediation, deriving both from the mediator's independent view and the party representatives' creativity.

The interest-based approach to dispute resolution often comes as a revelation to lawyers. Many see it as outside their comfort zone, because they have not been trained in commerce, or underlying finance, balance sheets, profit margins, cash flow and liquidity problems, corporate tax affairs, management speak, management time and opportunity cost, valuing reputational damage, or the host of factors which determine whether a business will succeed or fail, particularly if it is a young enterprise. By the same token few lawyers have been trained specifically in relationship counselling or inter-personal communication. So, it is understandable that lawyers may feel less comfortable operating outside the framework of the Civil Procedure Rules.

For transactional lawyers, mediation provides an extension to their negotiating activities. They are more likely to understand the dynamic of having a third party neutral and the opportunities this may bring to the client, not the least of which is a flexible approach to problem solving. They make litigators seem rather heavy handed.

So, the way in which you act as a lawyer in mediation requires flexibility according to the nature of the dispute and the strength of your client's evidence and arguments, your client himself, and your client's needs and interests. These are factors which may vary in priority. They may also determine the advocate's approach to who should be in control of the process. In particular, are you going to allow the mediator to be in control? After all, your client was sold on the idea of mediation as a vehicle for party empowerment in management and party primacy in deciding the outcome.

This may lead to an important question that hubris tends to make feel unnecessary, but which the mediation advocate should ask himself as a matter of course: do you think you know better than your client? Unlike litigation, mediation is a sanitising process in which the client has (hopefully) given you clear aims and objectives, and while you can drive the settlement negotiations towards those goals, ultimately the deal is up to the client to take or leave. He may balk at your advice to fight on in another forum. The mediator may provide him with contradictory advice to yours, stemming from reality testing or reframing, and in so doing reduce the client's expectations.

The process may re-define for the client what a successful outcome amounts to; or it may simply wear him down. These are common instances which you will learn from experience. Ultimately, whether you think you know better than your client or not, you must work together and you must accept he is entitled to be wrong, even though your professional inclination will be to protect him from the consequences of being so. You can only guide him as to the alternatives for which the law provides and offer an assessment of the risks and cost associated with litigation as the strategic alternative to the deal on the table. We shall discuss this later when looking at building your client's ATNAs.

The client may have an expectation of you as a lawyer which is different from his or her expectation of the process. Clients have a general idea of what lawyers do, and certainly what advocates get paid for in trial work. Where the advocate needs to use the more subtle communication skills that mediation requires, this will not be as familiar to clients as their perception of what fighting a case involves. One of the big problems that mediation has had in developing in the United Kingdom over the last 30 years, as in many other jurisdictions, is that no socio-cultural hinterland exists for modern forms of mediation, and therefore clients have no prior background knowledge in which to contextualise the 'softer' skills that the advocate needs to use.

The public have not been educated as to what mediation is, unlike trials within the justice system, which are regarded as the focal point of justice delivery, and they have not been entertained with it. Since the earliest days of print media newspapers have filled their column inches by informing and entertaining people with court reports. Even today to go through a TV or film guide without finding some kind of trial being used in a drama, in a major soap opera, or in a film, is something of a rarity. Trials are and have for at least 800 years been a form of public entertainment, with galleries allowing entry to view the proceedings. Contrast that with the use of mediation for a similar purpose and there is a pretty barren landscape, certainly insufficient for people generally to know what mediation is and how it is perceived. There have been one or two outings in television drama, but not sufficient to yet enter into the public consciousness.

As a result, it is very likely that, for the foreseeable future, the only people who know about mediation are those who have been a party or otherwise participated in one in some capacity, or who know of someone else who has attended one. Statistically at present your client is likely to be outside those two categories, which is entirely understandable since mediation is a confidential and private process, which accounts for a large part of its success. You could even say it is a secret, and perhaps market it to your client as such: "I know a secret way of making you happier"..!

But this lack of public awareness and absence of normalisation gives rise to the preservation of the idea that mediation is some sort of trial, and your client is likely to think so until you tell him otherwise. Worse, irrespective of what you tell your client he may think that lawyers should come into the room and demonstrate they are participating in the same traditional rights-based combat; and that negotiation should be advanced with some degree of aggression or at least firmness, absent which the client may see a demonstration of weakness and an over-readiness to make concessions he sees as unnecessary or at least premature.

Certainly, mediators do not want advocates to be positional, understandable as it is at the outset, and would prefer that the people acting as party representatives should adopt a completely different approach. But I am not addressing mediators. I am addressing lawyers, and I'm talking to you as a lawyer and therefore I embrace the fact that it's perfectly possible to approach mediation in a tactical way and get as good a deal as you would if you were acting collaboratively. I think the chances are probably less, but I am trying not to be judgmental if a lawyer says to me that he is perfectly happy to be known as competitive, combative or confrontational even in the context of trying to negotiate a settlement within mediation.

Recruiting the Mediator as you Transition

Whatever procedural devices are used to embellish the process, mediation is at its heart a managed negotiation. If we did not use the word 'mediation' it would still be a managed negotiation. You can call it something else, but it is still a means of negotiating where you have the opportunity to use a neutral person to assist you, and more than that, someone who is both trained in assisting negotiation *and* being paid to help you get your client a deal. The role of the mediator is far more subtle than simply the manager of the process or the chair of the discussions, and the reason I say that is that the mediator has an agenda. The mediator will do whatever it takes to secure the parties' settlement. He has no interest in what the settlement is, or from where it derives, or whether it relates to the original dispute, or solves the case, or even whether it is objectively fair to both sides. The mediator wants the settlement to be a lasting settlement if at all possible, and therefore will be looking for practical durability, and workability, but that apart, *there is no point in thinking that the mediator is neutral.*

I will say that again because I accept it is quite controversial.

There is no point in thinking that the mediator is neutral because he or she wants a settlement and will work hard to get one. The mediator has his or her own agenda, and it is obvious he or she needs an agenda because they are providing a paid service. A lot of mediators are reasonably altruistic, but a mediator also has needs and interests – principally the mediator has a strong interest in future appointments. Future work depends on having built a reputation for a high success rate, and in this context, success means settlements.

The mediation business is highly competitive, with new entrants coming on stream all the time, and mediators need to secure the next job. There are in excess of 15,000 mediators in the UK who have undertaken training and who are qualified to work in this country and probably no more than 400 are employed on a daily average. So mediators need to build a reputation and can really only do so by portraying themselves as or actually being successful in what they do; therefore they have a driver, in the same way as has every independent professional person who is a service provider – including you as a mediation advocate: to secure a happy outcome for those who are paying you, and thereby convert them into your unpaid marketing disciples. Getting paid is good, and not being criticised is good, and appreciating a good result yourself will boost your confidence. But if you have a happy client that is the best marketing device a practice can have, because your happy client will go and speak to other people about this wonderful thing that happened, which did not cost too much money; which secured a reasonable deal; which is all over and done with; and which lifted the heavy burden of dispute from his or her shoulders. You get repeat business, and you get new business. As a marketing device, that's free, unlike most other marketing.

It is true that I have been challenged in this assertion on ethical grounds, that the mediation advocate should protect the client from an obviously bad deal, which amounts to protecting them from themselves. But if this is a process of client empowerment and the outcome is purely the client's decision, I believe the duty of the advocate is to ensure, so far as it can be done, that the client is fully informed about the decision to be made, understands both the consequences and the alternatives which pursuing a legal case may provide, and can make such an informed choice. We act in a professional capacity and the mark of a professional is to pursue excellence on behalf of the affairs of the client by whom we are instructed, and in so doing put the client's interests above our own. In that sense we are not journeymen, and nor are we artisans. And in any event, we will recognise what is a good deal for the client because it is likely we are the only people in the room that can measure what is going to happen, or at least is likely to, if that deal is not accepted.

Reverting to the positive need of the mediator to secure a settlement, the advocate should take advantage of this driver to recruit the mediator to his or her client's cause. Do not concern yourself about mediator *neutrality*. Inform your client that neutrality in the sense of the mediator being free from conflict by an association or past association with the other side is relevant, but that apart what you should consider is *partiality*. You want the mediator to be *partial to your client*, not entirely impartial. If that means the mediator should in reality be *bi-partial*, and where necessary, multi-partial, rather than neutral, so be it. He or she favours *both sides* in pursuit of a settlement. This will be exhibited with care in dealing as the chairman of plenary sessions, and the scrupulous enforcement of confidentiality and the without prejudice umbrella that covers the proceedings. But for you, the goal is to help your client get an acceptable deal.

Therefore, a much more potent factor in developing the relationship between mediator, advocate and client is not neutrality, but *trust*. As soon as the advocate feels the mediator can be trusted, and the client also has sufficient confidence, the mediator should be regarded as *part of the client's team*, or indeed the advocate's team. Why is the mediator on your team? Because he or she is being paid to secure a settlement for your client. The fact that the mediator is simultaneously being paid to secure a settlement for the other side's client is neither here nor there, if you trust the mediator. It should not be relevant to you. Your role as mediation advocate is then to ensure that the settlement proposed is the *best currently available* to your client, as long as it equals or exceeds your BATNA.

It is inevitable, and I hope should be obvious, that to do this successfully you must work collaboratively with the mediator. Ultimately you cannot remain in confrontation mode, and you must change from your stance as a lawyer if that is how you prepared your opening engagement.

Whether you do this prior to the day, or during the day, is a matter for your judgment, probably on a case-by-case basis. If you develop a reputation as a collaborative lawyer or dealmaker that can be an attractive marketing platform for a particular kind of client or dispute.

Moving away from combat

I talk a lot about the role of the lawyer in mediation. Sometimes such a course of action takes on a life of its own. For example, the mediator may see the resistant lawyer as a drag on the process or as an anchor, already as somebody to be separated from his or her own client. It is wrong to generalise, but if the lawyer is particularly combative or confrontational, using such an approach as a default position for negotiation, the mediator is going to be quite keen to drive a wedge between the client and the lawyer, or at least diminish the influence of the lawyer over his or her own client. A mediator will have the tools and training to do this, and if you happen to be that lawyer, you will be side-lined in no doubt a subtle and polite way. By your manner and approach, far from impressing your client, you may lose both the cooperation of the mediator and control of your own client.

You, the lawyer, should maintain control, while operating as part of a team; and you have got to add value to the process for the mediator to see your presence as worthwhile, and want to work with you, and for you to demonstrate to your client that you are earning your money. If what I have said is correct – and you may well disagree – you are less likely to be able to do that if you are confrontational or obstructive. It is a matter of professional judgment, but you should be able to see what impact your approach is having on the mediator, your client, and the other side, and therefore what your contribution is to the intended outcome.

For a long time now I have been talking to lawyers about how they earn their money in mediation – in crass terms, what value do they provide for their professional fees. This begs the question whether the function of the advocate at mediation is to perform in the same way as counsel at trial. In my experience counsel or trial attorneys would readily acknowledge they prepare for a competition, and a casual observer might look at lawyers and see some elements of playing a game to be won or lost, which really informs both their mindset on the day and their approach to preparation. In my view very few types of factual matrix which comprise the context for the problem, lend themselves to this approach in mediation, simply because the more successful mediation advocate will have to make a proactive contribution to option generation, certainly before the negotiation phase starts, and probably when building the ATNAs with the client well before the mediation day itself.

I have been challenged in making this assertion. Certainly, I have been asked about the virtue of being confrontational – while still being polite – in the opening plenary session in circumstances where within the case you have a killer point. Expressing it in this way may carry the mediator, who has some expertise in persuasion, for the mediator afterwards to use it to good effect in reality testing. My reply is that mediation is actually a very sophisticated process, and it has a very different dynamic to the way in which you would approach running a case in court, so the question is not whether you should raise this killer point, but when, and how.

In mediation you have a number of options: you can discuss it privately and confidentially with the mediator prior to the mediation and seek guidance on when and how it should most effectively be raised. You may reduce it to writing in the position statement to be exchanged before the day. You may open it up in the plenary session. You can highlight it as an agenda item. Or you can get the mediator to carry it to the other side in the privacy of their room in a caucus.

You need to work out whether this killer point is more effective coming from you, and if so, you can choose whether to grandstand the point, or whether it will be stronger coming directly from your client in the opening plenary, or the mediator, with the psychological impact of being introduced by the neutral? Or do you fear that with anyone else's articulation, its effect might be wasted by using a voice other than your own?

This is an example of where discussion and collaboration with the mediator may prove valuable but may not be available if you have alienated the mediator by your conduct, or even by your degree of engagement in the process, or lack of it. It will still be the killer point you hope for and will potentially undermine the other side's position when it comes to the negotiation phase and create a momentum towards settlement through their discomfiture. Deciding how and when to use it will be an important part of your preparation and delivery.

The variable factors might include whether the other side is represented in the dispute or not; whether they are represented at the mediation or not; whether you think it is worth carrying this point to the mediator beforehand or not; whether you think it should go into a piece of writing which the mediator asked the parties to exchange beforehand; whether it should go into your opening; or whether it should be there in reality testing and at the beginning of the negotiation phase. You have developed by this train of thought a choice of six or seven places where that information can slot in after working out which is going to be the most effective.

However, being the most effective place to use it may not be where *you* think is the most effective. It is perfectly possible that your killer point might drive the other side out of the mediation. You may be sending a subliminal message that you are not prepared to negotiate. The opposite party may react by saying, "We don't accept that. You are obviously not here to negotiate. We are leaving." If you put your point in the wrong place, and you deliver it in the wrong way, you're not going to assist a process which is conducive to trying to find a collaborative settlement, particularly if it needs the creativity of all concerned.

What you want to do is to get as much capital out of the balance between advancing your killer point and obtaining a settlement through collaboration as possible. So, for example, it may be that the vehicle for doing so is to say, "We have an unquestionably winning point. We can explain it if you wish. However, despite the fact that we have a killer point we're *still* here to negotiate." Then the message comes across in a completely different way: rather than antagonise by saying effectively, "You had better do what we want, or we will beat you over the head with our case" you are saying, "We are confident that we will win, but nonetheless we think it's in *both* our interests to hear what you have to say about it, and see if we can devise between us the appropriate solution."

It almost always pays for a defendant with a strong case to say, "Well here it is, we are listening very carefully to what you have to say in reply", therefore you should not be so confrontational as to present yourself as not really open to argument, or to listening. You should balance that with an understanding that your strong position might prevent a settlement on the day but some time afterwards bring the other side to a 'drop hands' settlement.

I accept this is a risky strategy. Even if available, the experienced mediation advocate will know that the process is likely to throw up a settlement that neither party expected at the outset, and thus to embrace and contribute creatively is an opportunity to benefit both sides, to earn their respect for you as a professional and that of the mediator.

An overly robust approach may damage your reputation. The advocate who attends mediation with so strong a belief in his client's case that he is determined to prevent his client making any offers at all is wasting the cost of the mediation, drawing attention not to his tenaciousness but to his obduracy, and doing his client no favours in the long term. In saying that I have one or two people in mind! Even if such an approach leads to a successful conclusion in the case, it fails to recognise the potential benefits to the client from looking at the flexibility mediation offers in terms of commercial outcome.

One answer to this dichotomy is to prepare for the mediation on two alternative bases: that one outcome may flow from the merits of the case; and that another, entirely different outcome may derive from nothing to do with the case, but some future opportunity. I will return to this theme.

While there are advocates who remain married to the strength of their client's legal case, so also there are professional representatives in the mediation whose approach is quite happily to sit back and let the mediator earn his or her money and so allow the process to carry the client forward without much practical contribution. This will occur either because the lawyer is too lazy to prepare properly, or he or she does not know what is expected of them, or because they want the mediator to act as a cypher and get their client to follow unpalatable advice which the client will not accept from them. Presumably, that is where the client has more confidence in the outcome of his litigation than does his own lawyer.

During the course of the day, it may be very difficult for the client to appreciate how it is that you are sitting there, appearing to do not very much, and billing at £200, £300, £400 or more per hour. At specific times during the mediation advocates tend to struggle to show how they are earning their fee. I believe grandstanding by the advocate to demonstrate the value of his presence does not serve the best interests of the client. To be properly effective, reality suggests in this type of practice most of your work should have been done before you arrive: the mediation advocate should have a clear understanding of what the client is trying to achieve and have gotten himself or herself demonstrably in a position to secure such a settlement for the client before arriving at the mediation itself. If that sounds ambitious, let us examine how to do it.

First, by way of example, I want to recount an episode that sticks firmly in my mind. In the very early days of mediation in this jurisdiction, the early 1990s, I was representing a client in a professional negligence claim where there was no serious argument to be had by the defendant on liability. We went to the mediation fully expecting to have at least some engagement with the defendant. And we had none whatever. They listened to our opening and came back and said they were not making any offers. At that time civil mediation in England and Wales was new enough for both the mediator and I to throw up our hands in horror and accuse the defendant's solicitors of abuse of process. We said, "How dare you come to a mediation without the intention of making any offer....How dare you try to exploit the situation by attending merely to secure information from us which we presume you then wish to go and use to your advantage." I was absolutely outraged, since what was worse, my client was entirely dispirited and about five days later, against my strong advice, he accepted a very poor Part 36 offer which had been made before the mediation, and which we had not even addressed because we thought it was so ridiculous.

In fairness it may be that the partner of the solicitors concerned may have been highly competitive and enjoyed being confrontational; or he may simply have thought that was his job.

It was a long time ago. It still rankles with me. But, with the benefit of hindsight, I understand that the defendant's solicitors were engaging in a tactic which got their client what they wanted, and for them that was a successful strategic approach to the mediation which delivered a successful outcome for their client *in the litigation*. I remain critical, but at least now I realise there is no point in being judgmental about such tactics, since what they did was right by their client. (However, I would never again agree to mediate either with that individual solicitor nor his firm, nor encourage anyone else to do so.)

So, there may well be occasions where a confrontational approach – even though extreme – may be justified, for example where a defendant accepts liability but believes damage either did not occur, lawfully flow from such liability or should properly regarded as either nominal or *de minimis*.

Strategy, therefore, is not something that you should discount immediately because you are engaged in a consensual process. I suggest it does not matter how you want to act as a lawyer: if you think mediation is a process that lends itself to how you want to be seen in any particular situation you should not worry about offending the mediator, or offending the process, or trying to do something which the process doesn't envisage. Why? Because it is *your* process. It is *your* mediation, irrespective of the mediation industry marketing the product as client empowerment. There is no *obligation* to be consensual, but as I intend to make clear, it is usually much more beneficial to the client for you to be so, and certainly in the negotiation phase.

As I say, the mediation community likes to sell mediation on the basis of client empowerment, but from your perspective this in many respects is a fallacy: you are not going to allow the client without restriction to go to mediation freely to say and do whatever he wants. There will be advice, guidance and preparation beforehand. As a lawyer or other professional representative, you will still want to defend the interests of the client as you see them. Obviously if you're acting in the capacity of the client's champion then you are going to be much more protective of what you know to be the client's legal rights than if you are relaxed and you think you're acting collaboratively with the other side in order to solve a problem. From a starting position, that is the difference in approach between acting confrontationally – or at least competitively – and collaboratively at the outset of the day.

In the same way that both mediators and mediation processes are selected by you on a case-by-case basis to suit the best interests of your client, so you can vary your approach as a lawyer. If you want to be known as a collaborative lawyer other people will engage with you on that basis; and they will regard you differently if you want to be known as a tough negotiator. Your opponent and the mediator will have to accept that is the way you're going to approach mediation even if the process itself is not designed for confrontation, and the reason I think this does not matter is because neither you, nor your opponent, nor the mediator are really interested in *process*: your client is interested in *outcome*, and that is what you should be focussed upon, particularly insofar as you need to retain control (or at least influence) over the protection of your client's interests and therefore, of the management of the process.

Whether you are working collaboratively or more competitively, and irrespective of such a label, you work out with your client before you walk through the door the most desirable outcome; and you earn your professional fee at that point, understanding the client's needs and interests, designing something which is going to enable you to engage the other side by use of the mediator to get as close to the desired outcome as possible; but also being flexible enough to understand that during the course of the day things may change – your intended outcome may be replaced by another, either significantly less desirable or completely different. It may be something that you or your client simply did not envisage before you received information from the other side, or before the mediator reframes the situation for you, so that you can then advise your client. So, where it is appropriate, I do not think you should abandon trying to get your desired outcome by starting with a negotiation strategy which might appear to be competitive simply because you think the process demands it.

Reverting to the episode I used as an example above, there is nothing to preclude a party from attending a mediation and say 'we are not proposing to make any offer other than the one that is already on the table now, but of course we are happy to hear what you have to say and we will play our part in trying convince you that our offer is reasonable and your client ought to take it.' That is particularly the case where defendants or their insurers genuinely believe the claim has little merit or is worth only nominal damages. Had that been their approach, even at the time, it would have seemed eminently reasonable and entirely appropriate. What I thought was inappropriate was the defendants claimed to come in good faith with a view to negotiate a mutually acceptable settlement and ultimately, as soon as they went into private caucus, told the mediator they were not prepared to make any offer, and this without adequate explanation. The mediator was tearing his hair out because he could not understand why anybody should want to come to mediation and not make an offer.

What I can say now is that sometimes such strategies succeed, but many fail and will simply entrench mistrust and make post-mediation settlement harder to achieve in practice. In my view, goodwill at mediation requires a party at least to explain to the mediator why they will not or cannot move.

As advocates (and their clients) become more sophisticated about what they do at mediation, or in negotiating generally, and as they gain more understanding of the sort of pressure points around which it might be useful to build a strategy for the day, a range of possibilities open up which may not have been apparent when they were trained, or when they first came across mediation and were told 'you do this, and you do that.' Now that mediation advocates have developed both experience and expertise in representing parties and can work out viable strategy and tactics to use, it should not be for the mediators to say it is taboo to use the kind of litigation strategy and tactics that you would otherwise use in court in a mediation. That is the starting point. From there it is easier to move into a more collaborative position, since obviously the reverse does not work.

Adopting a collaborative approach will broaden your focus, and in so doing have a significant impact on the way you prepare both yourself and the client. The litigation framework by which you measure your client's interests then becomes a safety net underpinning your client's expectation, above which you have the freedom to explore things that you would not in litigation. Such a flexible approach enables you to focus on the other side's position. And in so doing, in assessing what that is, you may find useful a mantra that I have used with success for a number of years, both in preparation and the negotiation phase itself:

**How can I help the other side get what they need...
while at the same time get what my client needs?**

It can be both disarming and entirely unexpected to start your negotiation, or your opening statement by saying, "How can we help you...?" Doing so is of the essence of acting collaboratively, but using the question is, to an extent, dependent on knowing first, what the other side do need, and of course, what your client needs. To that extent acting collaboratively will require you to know in advance of the mediation exactly what your client needs for an acceptable settlement, and what concessions might be made in order to achieve it. And please note, this information may be a very long way from the pleaded case you are advancing or defending in the litigation. You need to know from the client the degree of flexibility with which you can work. For your own purposes, you may need considerably more flexibility on the day itself than either you or your client envisaged before you arrived, since the information-gathering and exploration phase may have undermined your client's legal strengths far more than you considered possible. Be aware that you may need to have a difficult conversation with your client, and one you did not think you would need to have beforehand.

Orthodox preparation requires you to answer the question 'what is it going to take for me to get the most desirable outcome for my client'. A more collaborative approach asks you to consider 'how do I prepare to work with the other side in order to get what my client wants'. If the difference is semantic rather than of substance, both require a view as to what the other side need and what can be offered to meet that need. The more offers you can put forward, the greater the likelihood of a settlement emerging at mediation.

From Collaboration to Creativity

The move away from the competitive instinct into a collaborative mindset can be liberating for the lawyer. Freed from the constraints of proving the legal case in order to obtain a designated remedy, one of the big advantages you have as an advocate is to assist your client in developing options for mutual gain, while retaining at the back of your mind the clients ATNAs – certainly the BATNA, WATNA, PATNA and on a more sophisticated level the RATNA or MLATNA.

OMG may derive from a sensible compromise of the claim once a realistic appraisal has been given. Or they may appear from sources not only outside the immediate litigation, but entirely beyond its scope, and come from the world of the client and not the world of the lawyer. They may include third party interests and other new relationships. They may be concerned with future business, refinancing, new investment, reinsurance, releasing restrictions, transferring property, modifying pricing structures, seeking a range of changes in supply chains, management or distribution, sourcing new product or components or raw materials. General or in-house counsel in particular may be adept at bringing about new and preferred outcomes if they have a deeper understanding of what represents the value of opportunity to a company.

However, adding value as a lawyer or professional representative does not always require a proactive contribution. Though it may look strange for you to sit silently and observe, when you are ordinarily hired to take the lead in speaking, the real value that you add is that even if you say nothing else in the room, you are the only person that knows what happens if there is no deal. Your knowledge of both the risk and the costs attaching to the claim enables you to measure the difference between what is on the table and what will probably occur at trial, subject to all those facts that feed in to building your client's ATNAs, and any relevant changes to the ATNAs you can foresee as a result of information coming during the day, whether in open session or brought to you in confidence by the mediator when you are in caucus.

Chapter 2
Core Preparation Skills for the Mediation Advocate: Building and Defending ATNAs

As I expect most readers will be aware, much of the theory surrounding collaborative negotiation in mediation was derived from the Harvard Negotiation Project in the early 1980s as a joint venture between Harvard Business School and the Harvard Law School. It was initiated as a study by Harvard Law trying to understand when and why lawyers settled their cases and to try to improve what occurred. In research undertaken for the study, something like 50,000 personal injury claims which ran from about 1956 to 1959 in the New York district courts were analysed because they were very solid statistics, and during the course of their research they came to realise that within the fairly high and stable percentage of successful settlements there were a number of typical strands in determining what was happening as a matter of system. They wanted to try and create a better way of negotiating outcomes for clients in which lawyers could participate having been trained to identify the core issues in which the clients were interested, rather than the issues in which the lawyers were interested.

One of the core principles in mediation advocacy – indeed, in any form of negotiation - is to make sure that as part of your preparation you have a clear understanding of what is likely to happen in the absence of an agreement, and the Harvard programme created acronyms or abbreviations to support this, the most well-known one of which is 'BATNA' which stands for the **B**est **A**lternative **T**o a **N**egotiated **A**greement: what is your client's best position if he or she or cannot, in the course of the mediation, get a deal required. This really leads to two things.

First it gives you a marker or a target for what is your minimum negotiated outcome, and secondly it gives you a walk away point on the basis that if you have confidence in your BATNA then you know that your client is better off leaving the mediation and trying to secure that objective outside the mediation either in litigation or in any subsequent negotiation. I say that you can do this after the mediation because the mediation itself may provide you with information that you did not have beforehand and which may have a material effect on your analysis of your client's position, for good or ill. You will have seen the principal potential witness or witnesses should the matter go to trial, perhaps an expert, and certainly the opposing lawyer, possibly the trial advocate.

There also may be a pattern of residual offers that were made during the mediation which can be used as a springboard for revised offers made subsequently, including, in England and Wales, the tactical use of CPR Part 36 or, where appropriate, a Calderbank offer. It is quite common that the most recent but unsuccessful offer in mediation may form the basis of a Part 36 offer in litigation, albeit with costs considerations firmly in mind. In particular you need to understand the impact of the last offer if it was costs inclusive, and how that translates to Part 36 in litigation.

It is essential that before going into a mediation you have a realistic idea of what will happen if you cannot succeed in getting an acceptable deal and it is a vital question that you need to ask the client in your pre mediation preparation. Although this question must be raised in pre-mediation conference, the client may not have a ready answer and should be encouraged to think about it. In many cases formulating the BATNA is a more sophisticated process than you might think and requires consideration of a number of issues that both go beyond the scope of the potential outcome and costs of the litigation, and may require input from a number of sources.

It may be on analysis that it is not possible to have a specific target figure in mind, but to have a range of possible figures. You will also need to accommodate a non-monetary dispute by looking at value propositions and money's worth. So, in the same way that we identify a ZOPA, the acronym for the Zone of Possible (or Probable) Agreement by looking at the range, in addition to establishing the BATNA, you will want to work out the 'WATNA' (**W**orst **A**lternative **T**o a **N**egotiated **A**greement) and within those two extremes, a 'PATNA' (**P**robable **A**lternative **T**o a **N**egotiated **A**greement). Some practitioners prefer the acronym MLATNA – **M**ost **L**ikely **A**lternative **T**o a **N**egotiated **A**greement.

The construction of your client's ATNAs derives from a number of sources of information on a case specific basis, which commence by looking at the subject matter of the dispute and expand into areas of possible option generation. Balancing the value to the client of a solution that might be obtained inside or outside the mediation process is far from easy and should not be treated lightly by the advocate.

Let us start by accepting the proposition that the client is not really interested in the process of mediation. He or she is concerned with the outcome. That is the measure of success or failure and is your starting point when considering the subject matter of both the dispute and what facts or material the mediation may access in broader terms.

Subject Matter

Specific areas of claim – liability – quantum

Presuming that the dispute either has or may crystallise into a legal cause of action, the traditional analysis of claim value commences with considering the viability of the claim. Whether advancing or opposing it, the primary assessment by lawyers will be of the chance of succeeding on the issue of liability. Experienced counsel are likely to provide accurate determinations to within a few percentage points, taking in the existence of a legal right or obligation which has been broken or interfered with by the Defendant, factual and legal causation and contributory negligence. They will have considered the marshalled evidence available and measured the chances of success against the evidential and legal burdens of proof. They will apply the same analysis to questions of quantum of damage involving the legal issues of scope of loss, recoverability of damage, foreseeability and remoteness, causation and contribution, and mitigation.

This assessment is an ongoing process. A cynical view would suggest that mediation is an ideal opportunity for the advocate to view potential witnesses on the other side and see how both counsel and experts perform, and therefore how they are likely to do in subsequent litigation. Taking in such new factors may well influence previously held views of potential success, and if the subject matter of the dispute is likely to be confined to the narrow compass of the litigation, it is worth trial counsel being engaged in the mediation. This approach also indicates that ATNAs are not fixed but should be regarded as entirely fluid.

Matters outside the claim representing an attractive own-client gain

The client should be invited to consider what might be an attractive alternative to what he is seeking in the actual or potential litigation without being fettered by the legal cause of action. This involves the client considering his business, other commercial, relationship or social interests, tax and property affairs and any wider matters that might convey a benefit that he does not currently have, or which may avert a current threat to something. This is an area in which the advocate is unlikely to have sufficient information with which to assist unless there is a prior deeper understanding of the client's affairs. It may require input from the client's accountant or the finance director of a business.

Money and Money's worth e.g. property

One of the most difficult problems to address in formulating ATNAs is a non-monetary claim. A key question therefore, is whether either the contested issues or the client's aspirational outcomes can be converted into money or money's worth. This may involve valuing real or personal property and may therefore need an expert to do so. It may concern looking at incumbrances – mortgages or other charges against assets, in which case information will be required which may take time to gather prior to the mediation.

If it is not possible to apply an objective or definitive valuation for the purpose of the ATNA, it may only be possible for the client to ascribe a value to him or her of an item. The difficulty then is deciding whether that value outside the mediation is achievable.

Entirely non-monetary but with objective value – future commerce; future reduction in debt/interest

Within the non-monetary category are those items to which a value can properly, and fairly easily be ascribed: future commercial relations, including modification or extension of existing contracts or new trading arrangements, reduction, restructuring or other management or existing debt, and the recognition of the loss of use of money i.e. interest payments.

Entirely non-monetary but with subjective value to client – apology; change in working practices; new standards

There are specific matters which may be of real value to the client that cannot be factored into the calculation of the ATNAs. An apology is a good example of something receivable as a matter of concrete importance if sincerely given and meant. A wider apology for publication may be required, coupled with an acknowledgment that an existing practice, method or system needs to be changed. This may well be a solution to an allegation of negligence that could rank equally in the mind of the client with financial compensation. These kinds of value propositions may not be available outside mediation since the Court may have no power to direct them, even against a losing party.

Beyond that, can you put a value on your client's peace of mind and alleviation of stress, both to him, his immediate and extended family?

Building the ATNAs

You will be putting together the ATNAs with the client. It must be evident from what I have said thus far that you need much more of an understanding of the client's world than that normally occupied by a trial advocate. The dispute may have been characterised as the breakdown of a trading relationship between two long standing participants, not untypical of a situation in mediation. You, as a lawyer, will be able to evaluate the likely success and the costs of doing so. But can you value your client's management time? What is the opportunity cost of the ongoing loss of business while the client is attending to the mediation? Can you value the reputational damage that might be caused to the client's business interests merely to be engaged in litigation, let alone lose it? Is there going to be reputational damage even if you win the litigation? Do you need to recruit a specialist business valuer to help with these figures?

Can you value the future relationship if it can be restored? Can your client be specific about that, or at least provide you with a reasonable range of figures? Is the prospect of future business likely to exceed the value of the current dispute? If so, how does that impact on your ATNA calculation? These are significant questions to which the mediator will hope you have a ready, even if tentative, answer.

Consider from where the information you need will come:

- You as mediation advocate [value of claim in terms of case outcome; costs]
- Client [relationship; time; reputation; stress]
- Expert [liability in case; technical options]
- Client's supporters [where to provide added value]
- Corporate Structure [line management; governance; shareholders]

- Financial Stakeholders [client's bank; mortgagors; creditors; litigation funders; insurers]

- Client's accountant [Financial stability or threats; wider business affairs; filed accounts and projected management accounts]

- Specialist tax adviser [options for structuring the settlement]

- Specialist property adviser [options for transfer, sale and acquisition; encumbrances]

- Wider interest groups [public]

In the context of this discussion, I must caution against the lawyer's instinctive approach to devising the BATNA, that is you either win or lose the case, with the cost consequences that flow from the result. Even working through the difficulties of determining likely costs recovery when faced with issue-based orders, proportionality, standard and indemnity assessment of costs, Part 36 and Calderbank offers, and any adverse orders, you must take into account the possibility that the client may not be able to afford to go to trial, or may in fact not want to go to trial for other reasons, including stress and the impact on his health or members of his family.

Plainly, therefore, it is not merely a question of you thinking all you have to do is to fight the case and win it, so that the BATNA is simply to fight and "win", secure the assessed costs of doing so less irrecoverable costs, and by contrast the WATNA is to "lose".

From the client's perspective the matter may be viewed very differently, particularly as mediation provides him or her with an alternative to the remedy of the Court, and potentially something the Court cannot deliver.

What we (now) know of the other side?

The other imponderable in formulating the BATNA is your appraisal of the other side.

- Are they financially sound? Do they have significant outstanding trading or tax liabilities? What is the capital structure of the business? Are you actually dealing with the true beneficial owner?

  This goes to their ability and willingness to go to trial, and more important, enforcement of any judgment your client may secure.

- Representation

  Are you impressed by their legal team? And if so, what impact may that have on your assessment of the outcome if the matter remains in or proceeds to litigation.

  Is the expert they are using likely to impress at trial? How is that going to impact your assessment of liability and/or quantum. Does he or she present a technical solution that is workable and attractive.

- Structure of governance – authority to deal

  Are there governance issues in the structure of the other side, if a business or corporate entity, that will make their tactical or procedural decisions more or less likely to be discernible.

- Valuation

  Is it possible to assess how the other side view their own prospects outside the mediation? Do you have sufficient information to attempt to calculate their own ATNAs? And if so, can you make a reasonable comparison given the circumstances.

- Funding

  How are they funding the litigation? Are they insured, or relying on a third party funder? Have they disclosed the existence of a DBA agreement or other funding agreement?

Using ATNAs in the course of the mediation

In one sense ATNAs need to be viewed optimistically and used robustly. They represent anchors or targets, depending on whether you use them offensively or defensively. ATNAs are essentially fluid because they are dependent on information that may change, and that change may come during the course of the day. In particular some of those factors to which I referred above concerning what you know of the other side may only become clear on the day of the mediation itself. That being so you need to make time to adjust, tweak and fine-tune your BATNA over the course of the day.

This is one of the important matters that should occupy you and the client in the privacy of your room when the mediator is absent. Any time you think there may be a material change in your assessment, re-open that discussion with your client and explain your view. This may lead to a direct change in your instructions. There may be a significant impact on your original evaluation of the case which the mediator may choose to exploit if he or she thinks it presents leverage with which to get your client to reduce expectation. It is wise therefore, to have a private conversation with your client in order to present a united front to the mediator.

Do you inform the mediator?

A key strategic decision is whether you tell the mediator what your ATNAs are, either at all, or when or if asked. You should seek the client's express instruction to reveal this information, which is, of course, privileged. That includes when it may be appropriate to do so. You need to feel confident that the mediator will not use knowledge of the ATNAs against you, and in so doing create a wedge between yourself and your own client. Many inexperienced mediators do so because they see a confident lawyer as an obstacle to getting the client to reduce his or her ambition, rather than an ally to use.

If it is a firm number, the BATNA represents your client's walkaway point but is likely also to be the minimum amount your client will accept. It is therefore in the mediator's interest to understand how it is calculated and to 'soften' it by the application of reality testing, a device commonly used to diminish client expectation, as mentioned above. If the mediator can undermine the clients' confidence in their present position in both rooms, he or she can set the scene for movement that will follow in the subsequent negotiation phase.

You should be aware of the effect of new information which emerges during the day on (a) the mediator (b) your client (c) any expert (d) wider supporters (e) financial stakeholders and be prepared to discuss this in private. The discussion may extend to the lawyer on the other side, the results of a private meeting between two or more experts, and other mixed private caucuses when you may likely have to defend the ATNAs from attack, criticism or change.

From a lawyerly perspective you will be aware of any new authorities that might have a bearing on the outcome of the litigation. In keeping with that, your preparation should include thinking in advance about where new information might come from on the day and devising a strategy to pre-empt its impact.

Chapter 3
Mediation Advocacy in Evaluative Mediation: The challenge of reverting to orthodox litigation advocacy

Mediation advocates who are used to the facilitative model by which most, and certainly all entry-level mediators are trained, need to understand and participate in, or, where appropriate, resist evaluation in mediation

First, we need to consider the issue of evaluation – what is the problem?

In the United Kingdom and many jurisdictions outside the United States, for the most part mediators are selected because at least one of their attributes is the ability to appraise, either at the outset or through the first part of the mediation process, the parties' respective positions, whether as lawyers or technical experts or as specialists. However, they don't. Typically, in the UK and developing mediation jurisdictions, civil-commercial mediators are trained at entry level to work under a self-imposed constraint whereby mediators are taught and expected to deliver facilitated mediation in which the mediator is prevented from expressing his or her opinion on the merits of the dispute, even if the parties ask directly for it. This is in direct contrast to mediation traditions in the United States and Pacific Rim countries where commonly, mediators, particularly judicial mediators, will offer when asked, a non-binding view of the likely outcome of proceedings as an impetus to negotiation. Organisations such as JAMS (formerly Judicial Arbitration and Mediation Services), which was founded in 1979 by Hon. H. Warren Knight in Santa Ana, California and now operates in 28 countries and has a panel which includes more than 400 retired state and federal court judges, attorneys and other ADR professionals, gives primacy to an evaluative model of mediation which relies upon the expertise, experience and gravitas of its neutrals.

As against that, the most important recent international development in mediation, the Singapore Convention on Mediation 2019, relies heavily on the facilitation of the third party as part of the Explanatory Notes to its definition of mediation.[1]

Sometimes more forceful mediators will give an opinion whether asked for or not. Yet we are shy of grasping this nettle. Offering a view on the merits, either in the dispute or of the proposed settlement, is seen as an anathema by a healthy majority of UK practitioners who have been trained in the facilitative model, whether or not there is a market demand and whether lawyers feel it would better meet the needs of a particular client in given circumstances.

1 Art.2(3)

If this is in reality a problem – which itself is a doubtful proposition - can it be overcome? Can using mediators who apply evaluative techniques make better, more prescient and more commercially minded outcomes which are more aligned with client expectation? After all, an evaluation by the mediator does not determine the outcome, even if it risks endangering settlement – it offers a non-binding opinion at best, otherwise mediation would be an arbitral methodology, which it is not. As to outcome it is merely a different approach to allow the parties a qualified neutral outsider's view of their positions in the context of themselves considering all their interests.

From the advocates' point of view, since this approach is within the orthodoxy of their training, is it better to seek out a mediator who will offer this facility?

Certainly, there are both advantages and disadvantages. To examine these questions it is necessary to introduce evaluative mediation in its proper context, or more specifically in its two proper contexts – first as a working, but hidden, part of standard form facilitative mediation processing, and second as a specially commissioned mediation procedure. To do so let us ask what does evaluation mean in practice; where and how it is used in alternative or negotiated dispute resolution; whether prejudice against its use is justified; and whether, having identified the difficulties associated with evaluation as well as the benefits, these can be overcome?

Mediation and Decision Making

Orthodoxy in the training and practice of mediators is based on two fundamental principles that have impeded the development of a more evaluative style of mediation in the United Kingdom since the inception of the presently accepted facilitative commercial model in 1989. From the outset we were taught the mediator should be, and should be seen to be, neutral. Any perceived bias is viewed as potentially a fatal flaw in the process, either propelling one or more disputant parties to leave or creating a risk that may happen. It takes either a very strong-willed party or one with objectively a very weak case to remain in the process where there is any perception of bias.

In addition, the outcome to the dispute must remain within the exclusive remit of the parties as a matter of ownership - the mediator must not be seen as imposing a solution – whether because his or her professional background engenders a mind-set used to operating in an arbitral way, or because he or she thinks a strong suggestion will lead to settlement, or even because he or she genuinely thinks there is a 'right answer' to the problem at hand. Even the suggestion of a proposed genus of outcome tends to be frowned upon unless it originates from a party as a contribution to the process, for example during brainstorming to overcome deadlock.

These two needs have driven the fallacy that mediators cannot and must not offer opinions on the merits because the process does not permit them to be decision-makers (a suggestion which cannot be so, since the mediator manages the entire process, in terms of participation, order of events, inter-party and party-mediator dynamics, timetable, and influence – all of which makes the mediator in fact a key decision-maker).

Part of the difficulty may be laid at the door of the lawyers, who remain the principal gatekeepers of disputes, and the way in which, as a professional body, lawyers have developed civil-commercial mediation to remain under their own influence. That is unlikely to change in the foreseeable future.

Lawyer mediators and lawyer mediation advocates tend to have great difficulty in avoiding an evaluative style, even where the facilitative process demands they do so. Often it is more a matter of suppression than abandonment. Legal training and practice are dependent on the structure of procedural and substantive rules, rules of professional responsibility, rules of logic and rules of legal thinking, all of which seep into an analytical approach to rights-based dispute resolution. In truth most of these rules came about historically as much to help protect professional monopolies in advocacy rights of audience as to help their disputant clients.

As distinguished international mediators Greg Relyea and Roy Cheng[2] point out:

> 'Rules may bring a degree of certainty but they also restrict possibilities. Rules may produce some defined standards but they also tend to result in generalised outcomes and remedies instead of individualised agreements. Rules, however arbitrary and ill-defined, may engender feelings of comfort, order and predictability. Working within the rules and also outside traditional boundaries of litigation, remedies and legalistic problem-solving may engender feelings of a loss of structure and loss of direction.'

But their impact is clear. Lawyers approach mediation from the springboard of litigation, or what otherwise would become litigation. The starting point is dealing with a 'case to be determined' rather than a 'problem to be solved'. This approach makes it extremely difficult to escape consideration of the merits while trying to move open-mindedly into the realm of wider party interests. And it gives rise to the idea that the mediator should be a participant in the decision-making process since he or she is regarded by the parties as a quasi-tribunal. These are the challenges that both entry-level mediators and mediation advocates are taught to avoid.

This is exemplified in two mediation scenarios: in the opening plenary session, the lawyer acting as mediation advocate will typically anchor his client's negotiating position upon the merits of the legal case or may have previously done so in a written position statement; a mediator will hardly interrupt an opening statement to suggest the merits are irrelevant. This will be because of either a lack of confidence, the need to give an appearance of even-handedness, a recognition that the dispute will stem from such legal issues anyway, or the need simply to get underway and get the process moving.

Second, should the mediator choose to deal privately with lawyers or other representatives absent the lay parties, all participants in such a 'professional' caucus will tend to stray back to an evaluation of the merits, even if not overtly

---

2 *From Gladiator to Mediator: The challenges for lawyers who become mediators*, Greg Relyea, Roy Cheng: Mediate.com April 2010.

expressed by the mediator. Sometimes – perhaps more commonly than the industry would like to think – even recent authorities in the particular field of law are discussed. In the negotiation stage professional advisers come into their own by weighing what is on the table against their perceived view of the merits of the case – in order to advise what will happen in the event the mediation terminates without resolution. This is the key role of the advocate in helping to build and then defend his or her client's ATNAs, and one where real added value can be provided, particularly in circumstances where the advocate is at a loss to know what to do or has been marginalised by the mediator.

This is hardly surprising, since most mediations take place, not just in the 'shadow of the law', as many commentators have described, but with a real prospect of existing litigation continuing, or legal process being issued. Participants measure their BATNA, WATNA and PATNA positions against traditional rights, remedies and norms that provide the initial framework for some mediations.

Why then, should we not recognise that evaluation can have a valuable role to play within mediation, and that even a facilitative mediator can learn to engage with and benefit from training in and experience of a more evaluative approach?

There are two aspects to utilising evaluation in mediation. Either as a genuine and important, though secondary (almost subliminal), part of the structured but flexible approach which we regard as facilitation in terms of outcome. Or, commissioning an evaluation from the outset as the intended primary approach – using the process to build a consensual solution around an expression of non-binding opinion by the mediator as to the likely outcome of litigation or some other tribunal determination, particularly with regard to quantum.

Using evaluation within facilitative mediation

There are a number of areas within the facilitative model which permit the use of evaluation to good effect, some without the mediator endangering his position of neutrality, others where such a risk may emerge but the circumstances justify it.

1. Merits and Reality Testing

Mediators are generally hired for their subject matter expertise. If the dispute centres on an issue of legal or technical principle, the mediator should reasonably familiarise himself or herself with that principle and recent learning on the subject as part of their preparation, if he or she does not already know it. Even without wishing to express an opinion, the mediator might conclude that in an argument on the merits, one party is simply wrong. They may have misconstrued, misinterpreted, omitted an essential ingredient of the principle, or may have been advised erroneously as to the state of current law, or current technical specification. If that matter can be clearly and easily demonstrated, privately in caucus, or better still privately in 'professional caucus', with that side, why shouldn't the mediator do so? It is a facet of 'reality testing', the only difference being the method of communication: the facilitative model only permits the use of adroit questioning to cause the party introspection. The evaluative approach enables the nettle to be grasped more directly, and rather more firmly. And if the defect is obvious, it can be presented as fact rather than opinion.

Whether it is a distinction of language or approach, the mediator should not permit the reality of the situation to be clouded by a party's self-delusion. Mediators must continually use their discretion, skill and judgment during a mediation process that is unfolding, changing direction and raising unexpected twists and turns. Gagging the mediator in such circumstances will be extremely frustrating for him or her, on you as an advocate who may require an objective answer which your client may then weigh, and which may influence the mediator's position in the negotiation phase. There may be value in shutting it out, but as a general principle it is difficult to justify general prevention where a mediator is sufficiently experienced and has the gravitas to provide confidence in what he or she is doing.

2. Dealing privately with lawyers or technical experts

Let us examine the premise that there is a separate and slightly different dynamic between the mediator and the lay disputant, and between the mediator and that client's professional advocate or technical expert. This stems from the impact of co-professionalism, or the fraternity between the lawyer mediator and the lawyer representative, or the expert mediator and the party expert. It concerns a shared familiarity with rules, process, ethics, the nature of professional instruction and retainer, the business of a profession, and experience, and this familiarity manifests itself in shared language and professional jargon, exchanging 'war stories', and the informality of professional relationships in the absence of the lay client. It may give rise to the leakage of pertinent, confidential information to the mediator (wrongly, or apparently wrongly) disclosed by the professional as an opinion on the merits, on his or her client, or a previously unspoken agenda.

In such circumstances how should the mediator respond to receiving information from a professional that he or she might not expect to receive directly from the lay disputant? The temptation to offer (or for the advocate to successfully tease out) an informal evaluation in such circumstances can be overwhelming – perhaps dressed up say, as an objective, academic overview of the current law in an area, or the current state of established professional thinking. The mediation advocate may be in a position to exploit such a situation, challenge the mediator's views and protect the client from bad news; or at least intervene with the mediator and know how to convey bad news to the client. In some instances, the advocate may be relieved that a mediator will offer an independent assessment where the lay client has been deaf to the views of his own advisor.

3. Crossing the line beyond reality testing

There are occasions when the advocate may encourage or welcome the positive intervention by a mediator in problem solving: two obvious ones are overcoming deadlock and appraising a technical solution.

Mediation is flexible but needs structure. It has well-established rules of facilitation but is fluid in the manner in which they are applied. Mediation is a dynamic, interactive and multi-dimensional process, which requires constant adjustments and sound judgment by the mediator. For example, the stages of the mediation process provide a template for reference, but they may be varied according to the needs of the parties. In some cases, there will be pre-mediation communications between the parties and the mediator, while in other cases, the mediation may begin with a private caucus instead of a joint session, and this seems to be a growing trend. Mediators may choose to meet with some, but not all, of the parties in a sub-caucus where it may be productive. Likewise, there is flexibility in the way in which specialised communication techniques are used by a mediator.

In problem solving mediators are asked to bring to the table their training in the mediation process as 'process experts'. In addition, they bring to the table their communication and negotiation skills and abilities. Mediation asks that mediators refrain from limiting themselves to strictly traditional money agreements as settlement options. They are challenged to be open-minded about the range of possible solutions that may exist for any given conflict. They are asked, in essence, to be flexible, to allow the parties to help determine the direction of the mediation process, and to allow litigants to find solutions that, while lawful, are unique to their particular circumstances and interests. The effective mediation advocate will recognise these attributes in their mediators of choice in order to maximise option generation for the client. Working imaginatively with both the mediator and advocates on the other side may create a solution none thought possible at the outset because no-one envisaged its possibility.

The other important area where appraisal is of real value is creativity in surpassing deadlock. When faced with an impasse you naturally look to the mediator to find a way of overcoming it, almost passing responsibility for the impending failure of settlement from your shoulders. You rely on the mediator's subject-matter expertise, his experience of other difficult mediations, the application of a supposed objectivity – reasonableness - to the parties' current entrenchment, and in doing so you are asking the mediator to go substantially beyond mere reality testing.

4. The concept of judging

It is an irony that judges appear to be the hardest people to train as facilitative mediators, lawyers are the next hardest and the rest of the population is the easiest. The law encourages judges and lawyers to be judgmental about the facts, the law, and the credibility of witnesses and parties. Often, the act of analysing these factors moves into the realm of sitting in judgment of others as people. This type of focused analysis and global judgment is a difficult habit to break.

A retired judge-mediator faces the challenge of listening with an open mind to parties who have already submitted compelling mediation briefs. A lawyer-mediator has to resist the temptation to make early and unfounded judgments about the merits of a claim or defence. Harder still is the task of suspending judgment (or disbelief) while the parties make persuasive arguments during mediation and the mediator observes characteristics in parties that would otherwise lead a person to develop personal feelings that favour or disfavour individual parties, according to natural or subliminal bias.

A mediator is asked to inquire about the factual background of a dispute and to entertain the parties' positions on the issues and applicable law — without making public or private judgments. In many respects that will be the starting point for the mediation advocate, using the pleaded case as a springboard for negotiation and option generation. Mediators are asked to treat the parties with equal respect, courtesy and consideration regardless of any personal feelings that may be generated. To the extent possible, mediators are also asked to separate their personal feelings about parties from the facts, the law and other circumstances surrounding their claims.

But both lawyer-mediators and lawyers acting as mediation advocates, by virtue of their training and experience, may tend to form early and rigid professional opinions about a dispute and the parties involved. In mediation, the challenge for the mediator is to hold in reserve the process of judgment, while analysing the case and facilitating communication between the parties. Evaluation of the elements of a case does not necessarily include a global evaluation or rendering of a judgment. Moreover, the manner in which a professional evaluation is conveyed does not necessarily require that a lawyer-mediator come across as if they are rendering a final judgment; instead, an evaluation can be described in terms of possible outcomes and can be the basis for a dialogue with the parties and their attorneys rather than a pronouncement. Mediation remains thus, a process of empowerment, even when the techniques a mediator uses may be invisible to the parties.

How to Commission Evaluative Mediation

Evaluative mediation is generally understood to be a process which may include an assessment by the mediator of the strengths and weaknesses of the parties' cases and a prediction of the likely outcome of the case. There must be clarity and agreement among the neutral and the parties as to what the process is to be and what it is not.

An initial problem is that parties and mediators do not have the same expectations regarding evaluative mediation. That is where clarification from the mediation advocate that has commissioned mediation on an evaluative basis comes in. Some parties wish to retain an evaluative mediator to help them get an objective view of their case and to prod the parties to reach a reasonable settlement based upon his or her understanding of their respective merits. For parties who wish to get an actual opinion on the relative merits of their case, they are probably best advised to obtain the services of a neutral evaluator.

Neutral evaluation (otherwise known as ENE) is a disciplined and principled process. The neutral is chosen for knowledge and experience and listens to the arguments of both sides, researches the matter and comes up with an opinion. Evaluative mediation is different. To the extent that parties believe they are obtaining a mediator who will also give a neutral evaluation, they may be under a misapprehension.

An evaluative mediator may or may not offer any opinion regarding the merits of the case. The mediator may make statements that imply to the parties that the mediator has an opinion. The parties may assume that the stated or implied opinion is based upon the mediator's actual knowledge of the law. However, the mediator is unlikely to do any research, and his opinion may be based upon the arguments as stated by the attorneys rather than any independent knowledge or research on the issues in the case. Or the opinion may be based upon a common-sense or 'reasonable' view of the matter if the mediator is not a lawyer but a technician.

Under these circumstances the advocate must exercise caution in commissioning an evaluative mediation. Both parties must know and agree precisely what kind of service they are retaining, and if and when the mediator is going to deliver an opinion, how he or she should do so.

The Mediator's view of settlement

One of the tools of the evaluative mediator is the mediator's proposal. The proposal is a settlement amount which the mediator suggests to the parties. It can have a strong impact since it is coming from the mediator, and some parties may assume that it is based upon the mediator's independent knowledge of the law and understanding of the case. However, the proposal may not be tied to any particular legal view of the case but may be a monetary amount that the mediator believes will appeal to both parties. Most problematically, the choice of amount will tend to favour the party who has bargained strategically, who has withheld information and who has taken a hard line. Yet, you will recognise these are the very actions that we want to discourage in the use of facilitative mediation. Thus, knowing that a mediator may make a mediator's proposal is likely to frustrate the facilitative mediation process. The two are therefore incompatible.

As I have said, evaluative mediation is not neutral evaluation. It is a different and more confusing animal. A lack of clarity on the part of the parties as to the basis of the mediator's opinion, to the extent that the mediator is only helping the parties explore the law related to the case as argued by the parties, may not lead to an 'evaluative mediation' at all. A facilitative mediator may feel it is appropriate to fine tune the lawyers' elocution of their legal arguments and clarify their disagreement regarding the law as a way of narrowing the issues and gaining clarity for the parties and advocates. A facilitative mediator would make clear that he is not bringing his own knowledge of the law to the task but is simply narrowing the issues as presented by the advocates. An evaluative mediator may be doing just this, but unless he is clear about whether or not he brings his own knowledge to the task (and if he is an evaluative mediator, why wouldn't he?), then the parties may assume, incorrectly, that he is doing so.

In the situation where an evaluative mediator is acting as a neutral evaluator, but is not being rigorous in obtaining all the facts or researching the law, is he really providing the service that the parties expect? The nature of that service being provided should be clear to both the mediator and the parties. The expectations of the parties must be made clear and the mediator must determine that he can meet those expectations before taking on the job.

If an evaluation is to be given or a recommendation for settlement proposed, the ground should be prepared fully beforehand.

Preparation

In order that mediation advocates ensure the parties come adequately prepared for an evaluation they should all agree that an evaluation should be made, and such an agreement should be well defined as to the scope and terms of any evaluation. This should include what the mediator is to evaluate, what the mediator needs to see or hear in order to be able to do so, to whom the evaluation should be made and the procedural consequences of having done so.

Any evaluation should be made as late as possible after all non-evaluative alternatives have been exhausted and to ensure that the mediator's knowledge of the case is at its greatest. The form of the evaluation – whether verbal or in writing – must be agreed.

The parties need to be aware of the implications, particularly the dangers, of an evaluation being given. A reassessment of the strengths and weaknesses and the no-settlement alternatives should be made with each party in private, and this inevitably means reconsidering the BATNA.

Delivery

It is recommended that any evaluation should be:

- preceded by emphasising the neutrality of the mediator, with a reminder that it is:

  - non-binding

  - identical to both parties

  - without blame or judgment

  - mindful of potential injury to the party/lawyer relationship

  - worded so as to avoid, or reduce, loss of face to the party or advisors

  - honest

  - impersonal

- delivered in private to each party using identical words if possible (although there may be a different emphasis according to the party's position)

- relayed as the best commercial solution, given the facts and opinions revealed in the mediation, and the limitations of the mediator's instructions on, and disclosure in, the case

- giving a settlement range to encourage further negotiation (and therefore ownership by the parties)
- given without justification or detailed reasons (to avoid parties being diverted from the settlement into discussing the basis of the evaluation).

What happens next is critical to the success of the evaluation. After delivering the evaluation, the mediator should give the parties time to consider and reassess their position, help them to devise strategies that avoid entrenchment or loss of face and encourage the parties into co-operative problem solving.

The mediation advocates should encourage the parties to see the evaluation as impartial data for them to use as a foundation for settlement. Leave the door open for the mediation to continue, or for a further day of mediation to be arranged in the future.

Post-script to evaluation – Do you really want to use it?

Evaluative mediation demands a calculated decision on the part of the mediator, in informed cooperation with mediation advocates, and should never be something that happens by default. To be productive rather than destructive, it requires a delicate balance of role and relationship with the parties for, once started, there is no going back.

The client should be made aware of the dangers of commissioning an evaluative mediator. While the above procedural guidelines are intended to mitigate these, it will remain apparent that the use of evaluation is likely to lead to the following important and natural perceptions:

- loss of neutrality

It is unlikely that an evaluation will please both parties, and it is quite possible that it will please neither. The result may be that at least one of the parties will see the mediator as partial to the other side and that, in their perception, the mediator will no longer be able to fulfil a neutral role. Certainly, there is a likelihood that one party will wish to leave the process, believing it to be tainted. It will be an additional burden for the mediation advocate to persuade his client to keep faith with either that mediator or the process generally.

- loss of confidentiality

The mediator is in the privileged position of knowing confidential information and the evaluation will be made using that knowledge. There is a danger that confidentiality will be breached by the information revealed in the evaluation. The mediation advocate needs to consider with great care the likely impact, both within the mediation, and the possible release of knowledge beyond it.

- loss of ownership by the parties

One of the key benefits of mediation is that it returns control over the outcome of the dispute to the parties. Mediator evaluation challenges that benefit, at least to an extent. While the mediator will say the evaluation is non-binding and the parties retain control of the final decision, the influence of the mediator will be substantial, and advocates will have difficulty in persuading their clients that the views of the mediator do not matter.

- entrenchment

Although evaluation may overcome a deadlock it may create entrenchment by one or all parties in their new position. Fairly obviously a party that has been told by the mediator he or she favours their analysis of the outcome of the case will want to use that as leverage in the negotiation and will strengthen their BATNA accordingly.

- collusion

A party may adopt the evaluation, perhaps insisting that it vindicates their position, and try to enlist the mediator's help in persuading the other side to agree. This is likely to feed into the other side's perception that the mediator has failed as a neutral and make settlement within the process less likely.

- loss of face

A party who has been committed to a position may not find it easy to 'decommit'. This may cause loss of personal or professional face, which, particularly in some cultures, can be extremely damaging and is likely to drive that party out of the process.

- injury to client/lawyer relationship

If the lawyer has been advising an outcome that significantly differs from that proposed by the mediator the evaluation may cause a problem between them. It may also cause a problem between the lawyer and the mediator, which needs to be avoided: it is therefore essential that the mediation advocate has a 'preview' of what the mediator is going to say to his or her client.

The guidelines above will help to reduce the dangers of evaluation, but the only way those dangers will be totally avoided will be not to evaluate in the first place! It will be tough, but most facilitative mediations do settle, and the result will be far better if the parties find their solution themselves. The client who wants an indication from the mediator is looking for validation and approval, not necessarily complete vindication. Sensible and experienced mediators coordinating their tactics with mediation advocates should be able to find another way to deliver what is needed in conjunction with an empathic approach that does not spill over into agreement.

Chapter 4
The Migration to Online Work: Practicalities to Consider

At the same time as mediation is being developed in jurisdictions across the world, mediation is itself undergoing a period of profound change. The concept of online Non-Court Based Dispute Resolution (NCBDR), of which Negotiated Dispute Resolution (NDR) and mediation are but a part, has been with us for nearly three decades. With the huge expansion in e-Commerce and Ebay, Amazon, Alibaba coming into popular culture in the 1990s, it became necessary to create fast, low-cost and essentially automated systems which were designed to deal with consumer complaints. The value of such complaints excluded the use of professional advocates, save perhaps in class actions for collective redress based on product liability.

Much of the lead in this area was taken by the EU Commission which, over the last 11 years, has produced four EU Directives and ODR Regulations designed to create an EU-wide framework for consumer redress using cost-free online schemes supported by public law rather than limited to the private sector.

On 17 October, 2023 the Commission issued an impact document seeking consultation on a Proposal for a Directive of the European Parliament and of the Council amending Directive 2013/11/EU on alternative dispute resolution for consumer disputes, as well as Directives (EU) 2015/2302, (EU) 2019/2161 and (EU) 2020/1828. In its Introduction, Political and Legal Context the document goes on to say:

> "Digitalisation of consumer markets took an unprecedented leap amidst the COVID-19 pandemic, with constantly evolving business models and emerging commercial practices making it increasingly challenging to maintain fair digital markets for consumers and a level playing field for businesses. The EU has developed a comprehensive legal framework to attain its objective to ensure a high level of consumer protection across the single market pursuant to Article 169 of the Treaty on the Functioning of the European Union. As a result, EU consumers enjoy a wide spectrum of rights affording protection to their economic interests and safety, while businesses can operate cross-border without having to adapt their commercial practices to different sets of national rules.
>
> However, for consumers and traders to benefit fully from the harmonization of consumer legislation, the latter needs to be strongly and equally enforced across the EU. An effective enforcement of consumer law is geared to boost legal certainty, increase consumer confidence, fuel consumption and stimulate economic growth. The enforcement of consumer legislation rests on two complementary pillars: a) private enforcement, whereby consumers harmed by

infringements seek to get redress before a court or through an out-of-court settlement, either individually or as a group; and b) public enforcement, which is carried out mainly by public authorities seeking to protect the collective interest of consumers by removing bad practices from the market and sanctioning the perpetrators.

This impact assessment concerns Alternative Dispute Resolution (ADR) schemes to which consumers may refer their disputes with a trader in a simple, fast and low-cost alternative to judicial proceedings. The strengthening of private enforcement through the facilitation of out-of-court consumer redress has long been an objective of EU consumer policy. In its Single Market Act of 2011, the Commission identified legislation on ADR as one of the levers needed to boost growth, strengthen consumer confidence and make progress towards completing the single market. Thus, in 2013, the European Parliament and the Council adopted both the Directive 2013/11/EU on alternative dispute resolution for consumer disputes ("ADR Directive"). At the same time, in order to promote ADR processes for online markets, they adopted the Regulation (EU) No 524/2013 on online dispute resolution ("ODR") which provides a messaging tool run by the European Commission (the ODR platform). The ADR Directive aims to ensure that consumers within the EU have access to high-quality ADR processes to resolve their contractual disputes arising from the sale of goods or services by traders established in the single market. It provides for the availability of ADR processes for all types of domestic and cross-border consumer disputes, ensuring that ADR procedures within the EU meet the same minimum quality standards, and it requires Member States to monitor the performance of ADR entities.

In order to increase consumer awareness and promote the use of ADR, the Directive Communication from the Commission to the European Parliament, the Council, the Economic and Social Committee and the Committee of the Regions also mandates that traders inform their customers of the possibility to settle their dispute out-of-court. To facilitate the use of ADR by consumers, the ODR Regulation established an online dispute resolution platform ('ODR platform') which provides a means for consumers who seek to resolve a dispute related to an online cross-border purchase to contact a trader and proposed to start an ADR procedure (in some Member States, traders can also use it to contact consumers).

Launched in January 2016, the platform is merely an interactive messaging application available in all 24 official languages of the EU; it does however not provide dispute resolution. In the absence of a reply by the trader, the request made by the consumer is closed after 30 days. Its use is restricted to consumer residing or online businesses established within the Union. The Regulation mandates that all online traders provide an easily accessible link to the ODR platform on their websites, as well as a dedicated email address, even if they have no intention to use this system.

> In 2019, the Commission adopted a report on the implementation of the ADR Directive and ODR Regulation, which revealed that the Directive had led to increased coverage of consumer markets by ADR entities throughout the EU. However, the report also identified that consumer and business uptake of ADR procedures was still lagging behind in some sectors and Member States. Recent data provided by national competent authorities in early 2022, as well as targeted consultations conducted by the Commission suggest that there is still room for improvements and that the issues highlighted in the 2019 report persist. The evaluation of the ADR Directive conducted in 2023 confirmed the need for its strengthening.
>
> Most stakeholders have identified several factors that hinder the use of ADR schemes, including the lack of awareness and understanding of ADR by consumers, low engagement by traders, gaps in ADR coverage in certain member states, high costs and complexity of ADR procedures, limited use of ADR in cross-border contexts, and barriers for vulnerable consumers. At the same time, the complexity of consumer disputes has evolved significantly since the adoption of the ADR Directive. In particular, online markets are influencing consumer decision-making to a great extent.
>
> These markets are characterised by a growing number of intermediary services, the increasing presence of non-EU traders and the spread of sophisticated techniques used by online traders to manipulate consumers' transactional decisions and influence all their purchases through advertising that is sometimes difficult to recognise as such. The anticipated rise of consumer detriment stemming from unfair digital commercial practices in the coming years is expected to drive more demand for fast, affordable and effective out-of-court resolution schemes. However, in the absence of an ADR framework that is well-suited to the digital age, many consumers may be forced to either rely on unregulated private online dispute resolution systems established by online intermediaries or forego claiming their rights in low-value disputes."

The huge increases in online shopping, with more anticipated, the greater sophistication of fraudsters and trading cheats, and a widespread failure of certain member states to comply with EU-wide consumer protection have suggested that the present EU regime for online ADR is now no longer fit for purpose, and a new Directive is likely to be passed within the lifetime of this edition.

In November, 2023 the England and Wales Court of Appeal indicated its support for NCDBR schemes as a form of mandatory mediation provided that the order made did not impair the very essence of the claimant's right to proceed to a judicial hearing, and was proportionate to achieving the legitimate aim of settling the dispute fairly, quickly and at reasonable cost although it left the type of scheme for scrutiny by the courts on an individual basis.[1] The background to the case was a Housing Complaints Scheme which

1 *Churchill* v *Merthyr Tydfil CBC* [2023] EWCA Civ 1416

the local authority wished to use as its preferred mode of addressing claims, rather than go to litigation that would be disproportionate in cost to both parties. Such schemes – indeed many other kinds of institutional consumer redress schemes or business to business schemes - may now be put in place nationwide and are likely to attract mandatory orders for their use before proceedings can be issued.

Be that as it may, the most obvious implications for advocates in schemes run under the broad umbrella of Online Dispute Resolution (ODR), which has been operating for more than a decade, whether generated by AI or, for example, ChatGPT is that professional representation will become redundant for nearly all small claims.

I therefore want to focus on the area most likely to be left to mediation advocates – online mediation.

The wider implications for the digitisation of dispute resolution are discussed by the highly experienced mediator, Stephen Walker, in his book Digital Mediation.[2] Like many others it was the pandemic that drove me, very reluctantly at the time, to learn to mediate by using an online platform, in this case Zoom®. Stephen writes:

> "Whether we like it or not online mediation is here to stay. The 2023 CEDR Mediation Audit reports that there were in the order of 17,000 civil and commercial mediations in the year to September 2022 and that within that...figure...64% of commercial cases were being conducted online."

He goes on to add that while that percentage does not approach the 89% of cases mediated online during the pandemic, the nature of the field has changed permanently.

It is essential, therefore, for the mediation advocate to understand the differences between a mediation which takes place live, and face-to-face, and one which uses an online platform such as Zoom or MS Teams®. Those lawyers who are familiar with online work, including some hearings and case management conferences, will I hope already have realised through their experience – good and bad – the subtlety of what can and cannot be done well online. They may also discriminate between the various commercial online platforms which are essentially conferencing facilities. Some are distinctly better than others for this task.

I do not intend dwelling on the advantages and disadvantages of online mediation, although some of the latter will become apparent as we look at the differences. For your client, going online, where suitable broadband access and hardware is available, provides an opportunity to eliminate the cost of travel and accommodation, and the cost of accommodating the mediation, and allied catering. Taken together this can be a considerable saving. On the other hand, there are many disputants who wish to have the mediator in their presence and feel more comfortable for it.

2 Bloomsbury Professional 2024

As a mediation advocate you have much more to gain by being physically together with your client rather than you both being online separately and remote from each other. It is much easier to discuss strategy, option generation and breaking deadlock when together in the absence of the mediator. That having been said, if you are representing your client online but remote from him or her as well as the mediator, the following I think, is useful to know.

During my course of training as an online mediator (again by the said S. Walker - *vir multarum partium*) it was suggested that we treat the technology as if it was a third or additional party in the mediation. For those of us who entered practice during the age of the quill pen and Clapham omnibus I found this rather useful advice, since it made me think about practical technical matters as part of my preparation. I suggest you do the same.

The first concern I have is protecting confidentiality, and generally the security of the process. The mediation agreement will usually state the sessions are not to be recorded by any participant. It may be obvious but you need to confirm the platform being used does not offer a facility to record the proceedings without you knowing. If your camera, or that of other parties, shows a limited field of vision, you should check that the mediator has a means of ensuring there is no-one in a room that is unaccounted for. Except by agreement, all cameras should be kept on at all times. You should call for a session to be halted if a camera is turned off unexpectedly.

If unexpected people appear in rooms – other than children, since it is likely at least one participant will be at home – their presence should be announced; they should be identified; and if they intend to stay, they must sign the confidentiality clauses in the mediation agreement.

It is important to have a technology rehearsal, either with the mediator, the mediation service provider or any technical service provider. Not only will you be able to check that things are working as expected, a run through will strengthen your confidence and enable you to see the best camera angles and lighting in which to present yourself. That is not a matter of vanity, but more one of perception about your professionalism.

Since the pandemic most professional people have been driven to use at least one video-conferencing platform on a fairly regular basis and will already have formed some degree of familiarity with it. But it is useful to have some kind of check list for the preparation or test:

- Internet Speed

Having the right internet speed or bandwidth is imperative for successful online work. You may need to test your available speed using Speedtest.net. You will need at least 1.5 – 6 Mbps for HD video conferencing.

- Microphone

Please do not leave it to chance on the basis you use your microphone all the time. Test the audio function between two different computers or devices to ensure the audio level is fine. Ask whoever is helping you to listen for background noise including any buzzing or hissing. This will enable you to decide whether to use headphones or not. The same applies to what you may hear from the other device. Some service providers recommend that headphones should always be used.

- Volume

Experience would suggest that people using a microphone tend to speak more loudly than when face-to-face, even though you would imagine the opposite to be true. Sort out acceptable levels as part of your test.

- Venue

Think about from where you will broadcast. The quieter the venue, the better. Most of us who work in cities tend to switch off to ambient noise, including fellow workers, traffic, building works and aircraft. These may be very intrusive to those who are either unused to them or distracted as an audience. And once you lose the audience there will inevitably be some recovery time needed to settle everyone's concentration.

If you are working from home a barking dog may be a problem whether inside or out. Consider the effect of electrical equipment – the blender or kettle in an adjacent kitchen; someone watching TV or listening to music elsewhere in the house; gardening machinery outside. Of course you cannot sanitise daily existence, but it is better to give thought to such potential issues rather than ignore them and chance to hope. For example, switch off the volume or alerter on your phone/s. If you have animals or children running around in the house, close (and maybe even lock) your office door; let everyone know you are on an important conference call and should not be disturbed.

The way you set up your venue may also give rise to disturbance of a more technical nature. Check well in advance the strength of the signal, which may vary depending on distance from your router if you are using Wi-Fi, or may be patchy in certain rooms due to the construction materials used in your property. Interference may also be caused by input and output devices such as a microphone and a speaker that are too close together. Apart from interference or distorted feedback, you may get echo which for most people is worse than a distraction since it may make effective communication impossible.

If a problem arises, have a second choice venue available, to where you can move quickly. If for some reason something should go technically or situationally wrong, it is better to acknowledge it rather than soldier on manfully and hope your client doesn't notice. All you need to do is address the issue, acknowledge it briefly, try to solve it and move on.

- Background

Separately from venue, think carefully about what your background is going to say about you. The stock images helpfully provided by Zoom and Teams are easily recognisable now, and there are only so many times I can joke about the tropical island background being a reminder of how London will look with global warming. Being above either the planet or the Golden Gate Bridge is not really suitable. In addition there is the curious phenomenon of blurred edges when you move in front of a standard projection. It is a distraction if you project an image that is unnatural.

Your appearance on screen will be the first impression that the viewer gets, that is the mediator, your client, your opponent and others. When you are speaking you want them to focus their attention on you, not on what they may see behind you. Stephen and I once had the benefit of professional advice[3] in preparing a series of videos on the business of mediation for Goodman Walker, and we learned the importance of choosing a neutral background, devoid of anything that might be distracting. That included personal objects, pictures, and the natural clutter we accumulate on desks, cabinets and bookcases. Since these are all familiar to us we generally fail to recognise they might be either of interest or disconcerting in what they say about us. I remember my first head of chambers having a large print of Edvard Munch's The Scream on the wall behind his desk. It certainly became a conversation piece. Fortunately, that was decades before the idea of video-conferencing came into being.

Many use the opportunity of online mediation to work from home. Projecting a professional image remains important. This is not an informal process, in the sense of its importance to your client. Think about what may look unprofessional, or your client may well get the impression you are not as concerned about his problem as he is. Again, remove from sight all clutter, including clothes, piles of boxes or books (if you are a hoarder like me), and food and beverages.

Waiting until the event to look at what your camera is showing may be too late. Natalie Armstrong-Motin, the well-regarded marketing consultant in this field, recommends you "sit at your desk and take a selfie or a screenshot of what others see in your background. Remove objects on your desk or on your wall that may detract from your company's brand. Consider designating one wall as your company wall. Invest in the colour and image of that wall and keep it consistent, even if your clients know you're a solo operation, they don't need to be reminded that you're working from home."

3 The excellent Sylvia Cohen, one of the UK's best voice and presentation coaches: www.sylviacohencommunication.com

- Camera

Unless you have the luxury of more than one camera, you will be using whatever is built into your PC or laptop. You are likely to have experienced the phenomenon that looking directly at the camera does not put you at the centre of your viewer's screen. The difference in angle is exaggerated if you are looking at yourself on a picture-within-a-picture, which shows a slightly side-on view (unless that just happens to be my set up).

It is important to set your camera at eye-level, and to both look at it and be aware of looking at the screen in a more centric mode. What I mean by that is to be aware of where to look at your screen so the camera projects a face-on image. Some people put a post it note at the top of their screen to identify where they should be looking.

- Lighting

I have undertaken enough zoom calls to realise the impact of backlighting or side lighting on how I appear on screen. How we light our face affects our appearance on camera — dark and dull won't make the best impression. Looking your best is part of your professional presentation, and it is worth some time in getting it right. Lights and angles are important when talking to both the client and the mediator. They are a feature of communication and perhaps the most vital part of body language that online work permits.

You are likely to have available a combination of natural and artificial lighting, and you may decide which to use depending on the time of day and position of the sun. You should use both, but in such a way as to avoid shadows or making you look unnatural. The best place to have your principal source of light is directly behind your camera, so that both light and camera are pointing in the same direction. If you need to enhance the light with additional lamps make sure they don't shine on you in such a way as to create a reflection. Do not put the lamp too close.

It may be that you can use the settings on your computer to adjust the brightness and contrast. It is likely this facility is available within the software you downloaded to run the program.

Protocols for online working

It may be that service providers have in the past created dedicated protocols for online working. Since the pandemic and lockdowns in various jurisdictions mediating online has become so normalised it is no longer necessary to have anything so specific. It is useful, though, to bear in mind matters that might help you, irrespective of whether you are mediating or just having normal professional meetings with clients or neutral third parties.

Since I have focused your attention on appearance, set dressing, camera angles, lighting and background from a technical perspective, how you choose to project yourself may be equally important. Merely because you are engaged online rather than face-to-face, why should that change your choice of dress when dealing with a client? Even if the image is one of only your head and shoulders you should dress professionally from head to toe. Yes, we had fun in the early days of the pandemic wearing a suit and tie top, with shorts or pyjama bottoms, but getting back to normalcy means respecting the client who will have expectations of his or her professional representation.

Zoom is televisual, so let the rules for dressing on television apply: Avoid patterned textures, stripes, checks, polka dots and plaids. Try to wear neutral tones or bright colours, which you should but not metallics and fluorescents which may not translate well on camera. Ensure there is a definitional contrast between what you are wearing and your background. Check your teeth, hair and makeup. Avoid jewellery that may be distracting or make disruptive sounds every time you move.

Apply many of the same principles of effective advocacy as if you were appearing at a live mediation –

Maintain good eye contact if you can. This is obviously less easy than where someone is present in close proximity. This means trying to limit notetaking if possible, and have your notebook and pen very close to limit visual disruption. If you wish to read from a source try to lift it to approximate eye level or write it on a piece of paper that can be stuck with tape near the camera.

There is a very small-time lapse between you speaking and the recipient(s) hearing what you have said. This slowing of things down exacerbates the problem of people talking over each other, which appears discourteous. Get the mediator to find a visual means of indicating who should speak next, since using the visual indicators for questions or reactions on Zoom are much too slow.

Remember that the online process will make the whole mediation feel slower anyway, with clunky movement into breakout rooms that is quite likely to need practice, without which it may break the momentum completely.

Your normal communication cues, whether giving or receiving, normally work with the brain recognising and interpreting body language. On screen, unless you develop a faculty for intense concentration, which will be reflected in tiredness after a couple of hours, you have not got full body language available. This will mean that processing information will likely be much slower.

If the process becomes slower due to technology, make allowances for that in timetabling with the mediator.

Work out the use of the chat box facility. If you don't like it, or find it too slow, have some signs to hold up to camera to deal with particular items, for example when you lose sound. "I can't hear you."

Get the mediator to agree to a fixed time for breaks and lunch. Consider the need also for shorter breaks. None of us can sit at a computer screen for very long without a break.

There are aspects of technology that are of real importance:

- Have your mobile charged and switched onto silent at all times. You will then be able to have direct communication with the mediator and your client - so private chats are possible. You may want to take the mobile number of your opponent. Switch notifications on your other devices to silent.

- I have suggested a dry run with the mediator before the day of the mediation. The same applies to your client and any expert that is attending. Check that everyone on your side is comfortable with breakout and waiting rooms and knows how to switch on their device's audio and video.

- Send all the documents that you want others to see beforehand, otherwise sharing anything other than scanned documents on your screen is going to be difficult.

- Speak slowly but clearly. Make sure your points have been conveyed, and that your client is focused, attentive and not distracted. Choose your pace carefully.

- Most of the work will be done with the mediator in the breakout room. It is likely he or she will be even more conscious of the passage of time with the other side not doing anything focused while awaiting the mediator's presence.

- Work out in advance how you can have a quiet word with the representative on the other side should you need to without concerning your own client. There is no corridor, loo or other convenient private space without having another breakout room. Remember the mediator may find it harder to keep the momentum going by quickly popping next door to offer some reassurance and then come back.

- Warn your client in advance about the potential for interruptions, technical breakdown, unstable internet signals, and the possible termination of the mediation by accident – it only takes one wrong click!

Chapter 5
Appellate Mediation Schemes and Mediation Advocacy

Structuring appellate argument as a negotiating tool

Many jurisdictions have established Court of Appeal (ADR) Rules or Mediation Schemes to be operated by the Court, at the direction of its President. In Nigeria and the UK such schemes have been embedded in Court Rules. It is growing as a trend, having emerged as early as a pioneering programme created by the U.S. Court of Appeals for the Second Circuit in the mid-1970s and is intended to give parties a chance to settle while their case is on appeal.

In July, 2020 Patrick Kingsley, writing in Stradley Ronan's *Insight and News*,[1] said:

> "Appellate mediation programs come in different shapes and sizes, but most are like the one employed by the U.S. Court of Appeals for the Third Circuit. It employs a staff of a few full-time mediators. The mediation staff uses appellate case intake forms to decide whether a case is suitable for the program. Parties also can ask the staff to mediate their case. If selected, the Court automatically defers briefing. The parties submit a short position paper and then participate in one or more in-person mediation sessions with a mediator. Lead counsel and a person with authority to settle attend for each party....
>
> To be fair, appellate mediators face an uphill battle. By the time a case is on appeal, the parties' positions have hardened. One side has won, the other has lost. The winner is confident of victory on appeal, as appellate courts affirm most of the time. The winner may also have in hand a well-reasoned and -written trial court decision. And, of course, by the appeal, both sides have sunk plenty of money into attorney's fees – which they could have used to fund a settlement. These factors do not make for great settlement dynamics. For these reasons, it does not seem to make much sense to force parties into an appellate mediation – as some courts do. There is nothing wrong with reaching out to encourage the participation of parties who could benefit from mediation. But forcing them into it often results in a waste of everyone's time.
>
> Even with these hurdles, appellate mediation programs can post surprisingly good results. New Jersey's Civil Appeals Settlement Program recently reported a success rate of over 40%. Statistics from other courts show some appellate mediation programs have settled about half of

1 Patrick R. Kingsley: Settlement is still an option – a primer on appellate mediation. *Insights and News* July 30, 2020 Stradley Ronon Stevens & Young, LLP.

> the referred cases. These figures, while impressive standing alone, are all the more so given settlement attempts were surely made in these cases at the trial court level – and they all failed. So it would seem it is worth continuing the modest investment needed to sustain appellate mediation programs. The settlement statistics also reveal that parties to an appeal understand that litigation risks and realities still exist on appeal. Affirmance is not guaranteed; there is always the risk that the court might reverse the ruling below. It could also vacate and send the matter back for a new trial, putting the parties back at square one. The trial court may have written a poor-quality decision, or its conclusion may be on shaky legal ground."

If appellate mediation is profoundly different from pre-trial mediation, it follows that appellate mediation advocacy will also be, at least to a large extent.

The appellate mediator should expand the party's understanding of their own and the other party's perspective of the dispute, their needs and interests. The value of the claim will have crystallised by the judge's assessment below, and the advocate can undertake a finite and hopefully, meaningful risk analysis: the existence of a court judgment may be critical in assessing whether a facilitated mediation is possible any longer or whether the focus has to be in evaluating the potential outcome of the appeal. It is unlikely that advocates will be able to escape analysing their clients' prospects for the appeal since the leverage of likely success or failure may be the only difference between anything that has been available, or indeed offered, as a vehicle for settlement before.

The question of whether the Court at first instance was wrong, and if so how that happened, is something I address below. But unless there was a patent error obvious to both parties, the 'winners' will have hardened their attitude in support of at least so much of their claim that has been found by the Court to be justified, presumably accompanied by an award of costs. This boost to confidence will be in contrast to the losing party, but the latter may be even more committed to invest whatever resources are needed to conclude the appeal successfully, including emotional capital. Neither is likely to be of a mindset to make early concessions just because the Registrar of Appeals has invited them to mediate.

Having said that, the parties' respective positions may have altered not because of the fact of judgment, but because of the delay in the appeal coming on, and what has happened in the meantime. There may have been a stay of the order below, pending appeal. There may have been changes to the client's trading or financial position, or a genuine concern as to the costs of the appeal itself; the appeal may give rise to a Pyrrhic victory if substantive relief has already been granted and not stayed. If the appeal is time sensitive or built around the restoration of reputational damage, there may well be room for discussion, particularly if you are working in a jurisdiction where the mediation automatically operates to stay enforcement of the judgment. Under such circumstances it may be worth considering mediation even absent a formal court annexed procedure. It is important to look for outcomes which are at least as valuable to both parties as either winning or losing the appeal:

the fact of the impending appeal may itself be sufficient to raise the stakes for both parties in terms of risk as to the costs of the whole of the litigation.

Options which are genuine alternatives providing the parties with better outcomes than continuing with the litigation need to be explored in advance of the mediation and are likely to require a creative approach by the advocates, *separate from focusing on the merits of the appeal*. Mediation advocates must do more than simply see their role as educating clients about the law and opine on their clients' prospects of success. It is likely that new information may have emerged either during the trial or its aftermath which may be the source of such a creative view.

In England and Wales the Court of Appeal Mediation Scheme (CAMS) has been operating since 1997. It began as a *pro bono* scheme using volunteer mediators nominated by the court. A revised scheme was launched in 2003 providing disputants with a panel of paid mediators approved by the court, currently administered by CEDR on behalf of the Civil Appeals Office. Although CEDR provides annual reports to the Court of Appeal, there is no published report on the activity of the scheme. It is a fixed fee scheme at a modest rate, and also attracts Legal Aid for those eligible. Referrals are made in cases where either mediation has been agreed or sought by one party, or mediation has been recommended by a Lord Justice at permission stage. Mediation is voluntary and can be declined by the parties.

After analysing the scheme in annual reports CEDR recommended the Court should insist that mediators have contact with both parties before the mediation; this apparently increased the settlement rate; that a timescale for fixing the mediation date within 10 weeks from referral should be directed so that the Court is able to oversee and prevent undue delay to the substantive hearing; that judges should exercise their discretion to recommend mediation more often; and that cases should be sent to mediation where the judge has recommended mediation at permission stage or where only one party has agreed to mediate – i.e. the court should not wait for agreement by both parties, in order to increase the referral rate.

Irrespective of the procedural format, all Court of Appeal mediation programmes require parties to enter into a managed negotiation where they are confronted by the power imbalance of one party having the benefit of a first instance decision which is now under challenge. This requires a special skill set to achieve a win-win outcome.

Mediation advocates engaged by parties who have been directed into such schemes will invariably be lawyers, probably involved in the court below, although not necessarily: they may have been replaced by a losing client. Even a winning client may want more seniority in representation.

Participants in appellate mediation advocacy will require knowledge and appreciation of the relevant court rules, and the use of court-directed mediation in litigation at an appellate level.

Unless the circumstances are both unusual and compelling, the starting approach to a mediation of this kind will still need an understanding of the basic principles of appellate advocacy in evaluating what may have been wrong with the first instance judgment.

Trial Judges[2]

Judges working at a lower level are concerned principally with the facts before them, and to engage in the adjudicative process as efficiently and, perhaps, conveniently as possible. By and large, first instance judges do not like to make new law. They tend to work intuitively, within general legal concepts and look for precedent only where the facts of a relevant authority and facts of the case before the court are either indistinguishable or substantially the same. Judges at first instance are most happy when the finding of facts alone determines the outcome of a case, and will avoid becoming enmeshed in legal argument unnecessarily if they can. If a trial judge has to consider legal issues, he usually first finds the facts, then looks at the relevance of a previous case and decides whether the legal reasoning in the previous case can be compared and applied to facts before him. He will not wish to make new law, far less give vent to any policy considerations.

Even the higher courts tend to shy away from making indications of policy on questions lacking general importance, and to the surprise of many advocates appearing before it, the Supreme Court is as equally concerned with the factual matrix of a case as the puisne judge.

Judges, like any other professionals, require both confidence and experience to arrive at firm conclusions. Even the most experienced judge may be troubled by an oddity or perhaps the general peculiarity of a situation with which he is faced. He may be dissatisfied with submissions by the advocates appearing on both sides. He may be troubled by a recent authority that appears to be out of step with his own thinking or a common sense approach to solving the problem. Or he may face real uncertainty as to what to do.

While there is no formal mentoring process, judges, and particularly deputies and recorders, are encouraged to seek advice when they need it, and, if necessary, to adjourn cases briefly in order to do so. It may be that they can seek the advice of senior colleagues in the mess over lunch, if in a large court centre, or to call upon a judge with more specialist knowledge.

Judges in the lower courts also tend to be conscious of the disapproval in the profession of intellectual dishonesty. 'Distinguishing' is sometimes an ingenious intellectual contrivance to avoid having to follow an inconvenient previous decision which would otherwise bind the court. There are many examples worthy of study.[3]

---

2 This and subsequent passages concerning the analysis of judgments are adapted from *How Judges Decide Cases* (2nd edn. Wildy, Simmonds and Hill) by the author.

3 *Taylor v Webb* [1937] 2 KB 283; *Rothwell v Caverswall Stone* [1944] 2 All ER 350; *Fisher v Ruislip-Northwood UDC* [1945] KB 584; *Brown v Davies* [1958] 1 QB 117; *D v East Berkshire CH NHS Trust* [2003] 4 All ER 796.

As a member of the community, the judge is bound to share more or less its common thinking and accepted wisdom, and indeed judges often express sympathy with such notions when they find themselves reluctantly constrained by an earlier precedent to decide a case in conflict with what must seem reasonable to the layman. It may be that a case such as *Howard v Walker*,[4] where Lord Goddard CJ was obliged to say:[5]

> "It may be that the law is not entirely satisfactory on this point. No doubt, it is difficult for a layman to understand why, if he is walking along a road and slips into an excavation at the side of it, he should be entitled to recover, whereas if he slips into the excavation as he is endeavouring to get on to the road, he is not, but I must take the law as I find it."

would today be decided differently for precisely the reason that a layman would otherwise find the law unintelligible or lacking in common sense.

The development of the common law is essentially a sophisticated process of refinement in which a later and usually superior court examines previous authority to decide whether the *ratio* of the present case falls within or outside its scope. It evolves by identifying material differences, great or small, and determining whether the rule or proposition in question applies to these, and if so why and to what effect. The application affects not only the decision in hand but also the prior case, since the process of the superior court is to affirm, apply, approve, consider, distinguish, overrule or reverse the previous decision.

Distinguishing your Judgment

For the purpose of evaluating the merits of the proposed appeal to negotiate in the mediation it becomes essential in your analysis to have a scheme or checklist of items that will assist you in assessing whether the judge can properly distinguish authority which would otherwise bind him.

Identify whether the issue is really a proposition of law or a question of fact (called by an older generation a proposition of good sense). In *Qualcast (Wolverhampton) Ltd v Haynes*,[6] both Lord Somervell and Lord Denning drew attention to the distinction:

> "A judge naturally gives reasons for the conclusion formerly arrived at by a jury without reasons. It may sometimes be difficult to draw the line, but if the reasons given by a judge for arriving at the conclusion previously reached by a jury are to be treated as 'law' and citable, the precedent system will die from a surfeit of authorities. In *Woods v Durable Suites Ltd.* [1953] 1 W.L.R. 857; [1953] 2 All E.R. 391, counsel for the plaintiff was seeking to rely on a previous decision in a negligence action. Singleton L.J. said this [1953] 1 W.L.R. 857, 860:
>
> > 'That was a case of the same nature as that which is now under appeal. It is of the greatest importance that it should be borne in

4 [1947] 2 All ER 197.
5 *Ibid*, at 199.
6 [1959] AC 743 HL.

> mind that though the nature of the illness and the nature of the work are the same, the facts were quite different. Mr. Doughty claims that the decision of this court in *Clifford v Charles H. Challen & Son Ltd.* [1951] 1 K.B. 495; [1951] 1 T.L.R. 234; [1951] 1 All E.R. 72 lays down a standard to be adopted in a case of this nature. In other words, he seeks to treat that decision as deciding a question of law rather than as being a decision on the facts of that particular case.'
>
> In the present case, and I am not criticising him, the learned county court judge felt himself bound by certain observations in different cases which were not, I think, probably intended by the learned judges to enunciate any new principles or gloss on the familiar standard of reasonable care. It must be a question on the evidence in each case whether, assuming a duty to provide some safety equipment, there is a duty to advise everyone, whether experienced or inexperienced, as to its use.[7]
>
> My Lords, in 1944 du Parcq L.J. gave a warning which is worth repeating today: 'There is danger, particularly in these days when few cases are tried with juries, of exalting to the status of propositions of law what really are particular applications to special facts of propositions of ordinary good sense'; see *Easson v London & North Eastern Railway Co.*
>
> In the present case the only proposition of law that was relevant was the well-known proposition – with its threefold sub-division – that it is the duty of a master to take reasonable care for the safety of his workmen. No question arose on that proposition. The question that did arise was this: What did reasonable care demand of the employers in this particular case? That is not a question of law at all but a question of fact. To solve it the tribunal of fact be it judge or jury – can take into account any proposition of good sense that is relevant in the circumstances, but it must beware not to treat it as a proposition of law. I may perhaps draw an analogy from the Highway Code. It contains many propositions of good sense which may be taken into account in considering whether reasonable care has been taken, but it would be a mistake to elevate them into propositions of law."[8]

Be aware that a court is more likely to follow precedent than depart from it, since public policy requires consistency: 'The need for legal certainty demands that they should be very reluctant to depart from recent fully reasoned decisions unless there are strong grounds to do so', per Lord Slynn in *Lewis v Attorney General of Jamaica.*[9]

Bear in mind that the law is tidal, in the sense that it has an ebb and flow, and particular cases follow a pattern. This is best illustrated where a superior court considers two conflicting lines of authority, for example *Henderson v Merrett Syndicates Ltd.*[10] Does the judge's action amount to a radical departure from an established principle?

---

7 Per Lord Somervell at 758.

8 Per Lord Denning at 759.

9 [2001] AC 50.

10 [1995] 2 AC 145.

Conversely, is the judge building a logical extension from that established principle? There is a positive desire to do justice in the case in hand, and therefore to set a new precedent if that is what the court believes justice requires: see *White v Jones.*[11]

The Court will rarely overturn a long-established legal concept, although it does happen: see *R v R.*[12]

When analysing the trial judge's use of precedent for the purpose of fair criticism the following questions should be addressed:

- Is the present case on all fours with the precedent: what is the extent of similarity or dissimilarity of the material facts?
- Do both cases illustrate the same principle?
- Is the authority distinguishable because one or more material facts contained in the authority are missing from the present case?
- Is the authority distinguishable because one or more material facts in the present case were not present in the earlier case?
- Is the authority distinguishable because the law has moved on? This is of importance in comparing cases before and after the introduction of the Civil Procedure Rules 1998, particularly in procedural matters,[13] and before and after the coming into force of the Human Rights Act 1998 in remedies.
- Is the authority distinguishable as being no longer 'good law' because society has moved on? The argument is founded on a contention that the relevant social and legal environment prevailing at the time of the precedent has changed: see, for example, *D & C Builders v Rees* [1966] 2 QB 617 per Dankwerts LJ at 626:

  > "...the giving of a cheque of the debtor for a smaller amount than the sum due is very different from 'the gift of a horse, hawk, or robe, etc.' mentioned in *Pinnel's Case.* I accept that the cheque of some other person than the debtor, in appropriate circumstances, may be the basis of an accord and satisfaction, but I cannot see how in the year 1965 the debtor's own cheque for a smaller sum can be better than payment of the whole amount of the debt in cash. The cheque is only conditional payment, it may be difficult to cash, or it may be returned by the bank with the letters 'R.D.' upon it, unpaid. I think that *Goddard v. O'Brien,* either was wrongly decided or should not be followed in the circumstances of today."

11[1995] 2 AC 207 per Sir Donald Nicholls V-C at 223H (CA) and per Lord Goff at 259G (HL).

12 [1992] 1 AC 599 at 614 per Lord Keith.

13 See *Biguzzi v Rank Leisure* [1999] 1 WLR 1926.

A precedent will not be regarded as wrong, but nevertheless may not be followed, where it can be distinguished because societal factual circumstances have changed since it was originally decided: see per Lord Hoffmann in *Lewis v Attorney General of Jamaica*.[14] Similarly a precedent, though correctly decided, may not be followed where related legal principles have changed since the precedent was determined.

- Can the authority be said properly to have been decided *per incuriam* for failing itself to take into account prior relevant cases? A precedent may not be followed if it is found to be *per incuriam*, that is, where relevant statutory provisions or binding case law authority have been overlooked or misinterpreted in arriving at the holding in the precedent: see Lord Hoffmann in *Lewis.*[15]

- Can the authority be conveniently avoided as being 'persuasive' only, and having no true binding force?

- Can the authority be said to have been simply wrongly decided? In *R v Kansal (No 2)*,[16] a majority of the members of the Appellate Committee held that a precedent may be held to be wrong and justify overruling where it is found from a practical point of view to be unworkable. Lord Hoffmann in *Lewis*[17] went so far as to say that a case could be not followed as it was 'merely wrong', that is, wrongly reasoned or came to a wrong conclusion.

- Can the authority be said to have placed too great an emphasis on fact 'a' when the present case requires an emphasis on facts 'b' and 'c'?

- Can the authority be shown to have an inconclusive *ratio* or *rationes*? This concerns the type of judicial spree for which Lord Denning became famous, or the presentation of independent lines of reasoning not touched upon by arguments, the hallmark of impatient judges trying to set the law to right. Such an approach was the subject of explicit disapproval in *Rahimtoola v Nizam of Hyderabad*,[18] where Lord Denning was criticised by Viscount Simonds,[19] Lord Reid[20] and Viscount Somervell:[21]

  > "My Lords, I must add that, since writing this opinion, I have had the privilege of reading the opinion which my noble and learned friend, Lord Denning, is about to deliver. It is right that I should say that I must not be taken as assenting to his views upon a number of questions and authorities in regard to which the House has not had

14 [2001] AC 50 at 90.

15 *Ibid*.

16 [2001] UKHL 62; [2001] 3 WLR 1562.

17 [2001] AC 50, at 89.

18 [1958] AC 379 HL.

19 *Ibid*, at 398.

20 *Ibid*, at 404.

21 *Ibid*, at 410.

the benefit of the arguments of counsel or of the judgment of the courts below."

- Is the authority based on an absence of argument? It is well settled that a proposition of law which passes *sub silentio*, that is, neither supported nor contested in argument by counsel but assumed to be correct without mention by the court, is not binding on future cases, even if the proposition constitutes a *sine qua non* of the actual decision: see *Slack v Leeds*[22] and *Nixon v Attorney General.*[23]

- If the authority has multiple rationes, is it distinguishable on the basis that the wrong ratio has been applied in the circumstances? A good example of fair criticism of an existing line of authority on this basis is to be found in the analysis by Lord Phillips of Worth Matravers MR in *Great Peace Shipping Ltd v Tsavliris Salvage Ltd*[24] of Lord Denning MR's approach in *Solle v Butcher.*[25] Another example of masterly analysis of a difficult and syntopical set of three lines of authorities was given by Lord Walker in *Futter v The Commissioners for Her Majesty's Revenue and Customs.*[26]

There are elements of the system of precedent which appear to have changed over the last 40 years or so. At the turn of the millennium this crystallised in the significant debate over tension between the doctrine of *stare decisis*, which underpins the system of precedent in this and all other common law jurisdictions, and the freedom of final courts of appeal to depart from and overrule previous decisions of their own which they subsequently consider to have been wrong or no longer authoritative where in the meantime the needs of society have changed.[27] The current position is that the Supreme Court of the United Kingdom is able to deviate from its earlier decisions, although in practice it rarely does so. The Judicial Committee of the Privy Council in *Lewis v Attorney General of Jamaica*[28] and the House of Lords in *R v Kansal (No. 2)*[29] raised for debate principles which should guide a court of final appeal in contemplation of replacing its own wrongly decided precedents.

The Appellate Committee of the House of Lords had considerations which did not apply to lesser tribunals – the policy decisions that provide certainty to both the legal and wider community, especially in commerce, property rights, and the provision of remedies for changing social attitudes and needs.

The operation of precedent is therefore not constant, and sometimes not consistent: despite extensive electronic data retrieval and other support it remains impossible to guarantee that judges can know every reported case.

---

22 [1923] 1 Ch 431 per Lord Sterndale at 451.
23 [1931] AC 184 HL per Viscount Dunedin at 190.
24 [2002] EWCA Civ 1407 at [95]–[161].
25 [1950] 1 KB 671 CA.
26 [2013] UKSC 26.
27 See Professor BV Harris, 'Final Appellate Courts Overruling Their Own 'Wrong' Precedents: The Ongoing Search for Principle' (2002) 118 LQR 408.
28 [2001] AC 50.
29 [2001] 3 WLR 1562.

They still depend very largely on counsel for citation of all relevant authority, and quite rightly so in view of the pressure upon their time. Counsel are not infallible, particularly with the enormous growth in the law itself, not merely law reporting. Sometimes this may result in a judge arriving at a conclusion which might have been quite different if a particular authority had been before him. That decision stands, and may be followed in other cases until, perhaps years later, the point comes before a higher court where the neglected authority is discovered and the clock must be put back.

Criticising a Judgment Fairly

Successful appellate advocacy requires clear thinking, intellectual application and effective argument. In order to persuade an appellate tribunal that the judge below was wrong, you must understand yourself why he was wrong, be able to demonstrate that fact with clarity, and withstand a rigorous testing of your contention. You must be prepared for reality testing by analogy and hypothesis, by reduction or expansion of your argument, and by purposive analysis; and you must be able to show the appellate tribunal that your criticism of the judge is fair, and that it is right or just that the appeal should succeed. You should be conscious not only of the judge's error, but also of the merits of your client's own position. If you do not keep the merits firmly in mind, the court will.

However great the error into which the first instance tribunal has fallen, whatever the departure from canon, if the merits are not with you, then your case will be found to be, on the facts, an aberration or an exception to the guiding principle, and whether intellectually sound or by sleight of hand, you will lose. You may win the argument, but you will lose the appeal.

Working out how to criticise a judgment fairly requires close analytical reading. It involves giving an exacting consideration to the text and calls for a five-stage process:

- Reading actively.
- Developing a close understanding.
- Making a critical judgment.
- Understanding why you disagree.
- Forming a structured reply.

Active reading entails not blandly accepting what is being said. It requires an alertness in which the reader is prepared to challenge the writer to persuade him of the correctness of his position. It is unlike a passive operation in which information is absorbed without applying any critical faculty. You should remember that while grammatical and logical skill in writing clearly and intelligibly has merit in itself, the aim of a judgment is also to convince or persuade. The judge may use rhetorical or literary techniques, or the plainest of common language. Whatever the devices, they are intended to justify his findings. Your task is to react critically to the attempt to persuade. And much the same can be said of preparing to negotiate within the mediation.

The writer seeks to achieve intelligibility in his work and to convey understanding to his reader. The lawyer must achieve understanding before he can properly criticise. It may be that on occasion your judge is so prolix or diffuse that you have to strip away verbiage in order to search for understanding, but understand you must. As Mortimer Adler suggests in his work on active reading,[30] you must be able to say with reasonable certainty 'I understand' before you can say 'I agree', 'I disagree' or 'I suspend judgment'. These three remarks exhaust all the critical positions you can take. However, you should bear in mind that criticism does not mean merely to disagree. To agree is just as much an exercise of critical judgment as disagreement. Suspending judgment is also an act of criticism: it is taking a position that something has not been shown or proven, which is highly pertinent to forensic analysis.

You must understand why you disagree, because your disagreement must be purposive if it is to enable you to appeal successfully. What is at stake is persuading an appellate tribunal that the basis of the disagreement – or the criticism of the judge's judgment – is sufficiently causative or relevant or important first that the appeal should be permitted to be heard, and second, to succeed. An appeal is a futile – and expensive and time-consuming – agitation unless undertaken with the hope that it may either succeed before the court or at least lead to the resolution of an issue between the parties. Disagreement for its own sake is not enough: the costs regime is designed to deter criticism of judicial performance unless it not only has merit but will also be of practical significance. If other practical outcomes are possible, the Court of Appeal also actively promotes the use of its mediation scheme. That is why there may be sensible negotiation to be had where the appeal is regarded as a ploy by a respondent who is interested in achieving something other than the judgment he has already obtained.

Forming a structured reply will enable you to marshal your thought processes at the earliest stage, perhaps for the appellant well before you are called upon to advise or settle a notice of appeal and skeleton argument in support, and for the respondent what options for client gains are available within the annexed mediation. For the appellant, once you have identified the basis for your criticism, you need to formulate an argument that enables the appellate tribunal to understand not only why the judge's finding is wrong, but also why your client's desired outcome is to be preferred.

Analysing Your Disagreement Objectively

You have concluded that the judgment may properly and fairly be criticised. Next try to consider the position objectively as an outsider as, in this case, the appellate tribunal would. This is no doubt difficult in view of the two subjective opening positions. You believe that the judge was wrong. However, the appellate tribunal will instinctively start from a defensive point of view, wishing to protect the reputation and dignity of the court under attack, unless by some oversight or procedural defect it is fairly obvious that no reasonable tribunal could have come to the conclusion being appealed against. Taking a step back and making sure that you believe your criticism of the judge is

30 Mortimer J Adler and Charles Van Doren, *How to Read a Book* (Touchstone/Simon & Schuster, 1972), p 142.

reasonable, and that you are not just acting disputatiously or contentiously, may overcome this difficulty.

Consider whether the substance of your criticism concerns genuine knowledge, and not mere personal opinion. If the latter, then, for the most part, such disagreements may be more apparent than real. If the criticism has real substance it must concern genuine issues of fact and reason.

Distinguishing Between Knowledge and Opinion

If the judge does not provide reasoning or support for his propositions, they can properly be treated as personal opinions only on his part. While it is facile to say that all judgments are only the personal opinion of the judge, for appellate purposes it is vitally important to distinguish between the reasoned statement of knowledge and the flat expression of personal opinion. Critical obligations should be taken seriously: the practitioner must do more than make judgments of agreement and disagreement. He must have adequate reasons for doing so which can be justified in fact or law.

In this respect you must realise and accept that most judicial knowledge is not absolute. Knowledge consist of opinions which can be defended, opinions for which there is evidential or legal support of one kind or another. Knowledge in this sense is something we can convince others of what we know, or more particularly what can be proven to the appropriate standard. Mere opinion, on the other hand, is unsupported judgment. What is required is evidence or reason for a statement over and above personal feeling or prejudice: objective evidence that other reasonable men are likely to accept.[31] In dealing with an appellate tribunal, you will be engaged in intelligent controversy and challenged not only to carry your own argument but also to deal with the arguments of the tribunal itself.

The Focus of Your Criticism

The judge is making judgments about the world in which we live in the context of the facts of the case. His findings as to the facts in dispute give us knowledge or tell us what things exist, the way they behave and what should be done. He can be either right or wrong. His position is justified only to the extent that his findings are probable in the light of the evidence; were that not so, it may be contended that his conclusion is unfounded.

Much inevitably turns on your understanding with precision the judge's meaning, otherwise your disagreement may be irrelevant: an error of understanding in what he is saying may render the opposite argument without merit. If your criticism is founded upon a misapprehension, the appellate process will be an expensive failure. Issues about matters of fact or policy – the way things are or should be – are real only when they are based upon a common understanding of what is being said. Agreement about the use of words is an indispensable condition for genuine agreement or disagreement about the facts under discussion.[32] You must therefore ensure, as objectively

31 See *ibid,* pp 149, 150.

32 *Ibid* p 153.

as possible, that there is a real and significant issue at stake which can be readily identified, and is irresolvable without the mechanism of an appeal.

The Mechanics of Fair Criticism[33]

There are principally four ways in which a judgment can be adversely but fairly criticised: that the judge was uninformed; that he was misinformed; that his approach was illogical in the sense that his reasoning was not cogent; or that his analysis of either the facts or the law was not complete. These four categories are not exhaustive, but they cover most points that are likely to arise. Nor are the defects they describe mutually exclusive.

You cannot mount a sound challenge without being definite and precise about the respect in which the judgment is uninformed or misinformed or illogical, since it is most unlikely that judges of the calibre engaged in our courts and tribunals will be uninformed and misinformed about everything, or else totally illogical.

Uninformed

The judge lacks some piece of knowledge that is relevant to the problem he is trying to solve. You must yourself be able to state a piece of knowledge or information missing, show its relevance and show how the conclusion would be different. This is often reflected in such criticism of the judge below by the Court of Appeal, as for example given here by Scott Baker J in *In re Rhondda Waste Disposal Ltd*:[34]

> "In my judgment the judge was in error in the exercise of his discretion. He should not have regarded the interests of the creditors of the company as trumping all other considerations. He failed to take into account and give due weight to the evidence of Mr Weare. Furthermore, in the event of conviction, there is a statutory obligation on the court fixing the amount of any fine to take account of all the circumstances including the financial circumstances of the company: see section 18(3) of the Criminal Justice Act 1991.
>
> 43. I consider there were compelling reasons why leave should have been given in this case. The purpose of licensing is to ensure that the disposal of controlled waste does not give rise to: (i) pollution of the environment; (ii) harm to human health and; (iii) serious detriment to the amenities of the locality."

Equally the trial judge's analysis of law may be called into question, as did Lord Denning MR here in *Heywood v Wellers*:[35]

> "Now I think the judge was in error in thinking that the solicitors were entitled to recover any costs at all. There are two reasons. In the first place, the contract of the solicitors was an entire contract which they

33 This passage, from the first edition of this work, is also reproduced in *Effective Written Advocacy – A Guide for Practitioners* (2nd edn Wildy, Simmonds and Hill) by the author.
34 [2001] Ch 57 CA per at 71[42].
35 [1976] QB 446 at 458.

were bound to carry on to the end; and, not having done so, they were not entitled to any costs: see *Underwood, Son & Piper v Lewis* [1894] 2 Q.B. 306. The law as to entire contract was put vividly by Sir George Jessel M.R., in *In re Hall & Barker* (1878) 9 Ch.D. 538, 545:

> 'If a man engages to carry a box of cigars from London to Birmingham, it is an entire contract, and he cannot throw the cigars out of the carriage half-way there, and ask for half the money; or if a shoemaker agrees to make a pair of shoes, he cannot offer you one shoe and ask you to pay one half the price.'

In the second place, the work which they did do was useless. It did nothing to forward the object which the client had in view. It did nothing to protect her from molestation. It being thus useless, they can recover nothing for it: see *Hill v Featherstonhaugh* (1831) 7 Bing. 569, when Tindal C.J. said, at pp. 571–572:

> ' . . . if an attorney, through inadvertence or inexperience, – for I impute no improper motive to the plaintiff – incurs trouble which is useless to his client, he cannot make it a subject of remuneration . . . could a bricklayer, who had placed a wall in such a position as to be liable to fall, charge his employer for such an erection?'

Clearly not. So the solicitors were entitled to nothing for costs: and Mrs. Heywood could recover the £175 as money paid on a consideration which had wholly failed. She was, therefore, entitled to recover it as of right."

Misinformed

Here he asserts that which is not the case, that is, the judge makes findings or assertions contrary to fact. The judgment proposes as true or more probable that which is in fact false or less probable; it is based on a claim to have knowledge he does not possess. This was the focus of criticism by Lord Justice Stocker in the Court of Appeal of the trial judge in one of the actions arising out the Hillsborough disaster:

> "To summarise, in my view, the law is that, save in exceptional circumstances, only those within the parent/spouse relationship can recover damages for psychiatric shock sustained by a plaintiff not himself involved as a victim. This defines the category. The exceptions considered on a case to case basis are limited to relatives who meet the criteria of that relationship and who are present at the scene or its immediate aftermath. What has to be foreseeable is that someone may be present at the scene or its immediate aftermath who possesses that love and affection which a parent/spouse is assumed to possess, even if in fact that relative is less closely related to the victim than a parent or spouse. It does not seem to me that such a formulation causes any particular difficulty – it is a slight reformulation of the test of foreseeability to meet the cases referred to by Lord Wilberforce, not any change or addition to what has to be foreseeable in the case of a parent/spouse who suffers psychiatric injury by shock. The judge found that in the case before him brother

> and sister were entitled to recover. He did so, if I correctly interpret his judgment, by reference to the circumstances of the Hillsborough disaster and by the relationship which might be expected in most cases between brother and sister. He did not carry out any close scrutiny by reference to the love and affection in fact to be attributed to them, having regard in particular to any care (in the sense of custody or maintenance) which they had performed. It may be that had such a scrutiny been carried out, the facts might have entitled them to recover damages and the extension in their favour be justified under the principles enunciated by Lord Wilberforce. I therefore consider that the judge was in error in holding that in the circumstances of the case before him he could regard the brothers and sisters as within the relationship which would entitle them to claim damages."[36]

This kind of defect is only relevant if it is causative in the sense that it affects the judge's conclusions and ultimate position; see, for example, the child abduction case *B v B*:[37]

> "In support of the judge's finding that the removal was not unlawful, Mr. Warnock for the mother submits that the court should apply a strict and restricted interpretation of the term 'rights of custody.' Since the court had ordered interim custody in favour of the mother (subject to access by the father pending the substantive hearing) there could be no right of custody in any person or body other than the mother. Therefore, he says, she was not in breach of any right vested in the husband, or, indeed, in the court when she removed the child on 3 July 1991.
>
> I find that submission unacceptable. In my view this was the plainest example of an unlawful removal. The mother herself appears to have thought so, for she later stated that she regretted having taken that step at that time. It is suggested that she did not appreciate the legal position, although she was in receipt of legal advice at the time. It seems to me that the court itself had a right of custody at this time in the sense that it had the right to determine the child's place of residence, and it was in breach of that right that the mother removed the child from its place of habitual residence. I should say that there has never been any issue as to the fact that the child's habitual residence was at all material time in Ontario. Accordingly, I am of the view that the judge was in error when he decided that the removal of the child was not unlawful."

You must be able to argue the truth or greater probability of a position contrary to that of the judge. It should follow as a matter of logic that whenever he is misinformed in one respect, he will also be uninformed in the same respect.

Illogical

The judge has committed a fallacy in reasoning. This problem generally stems from two sources. Either the judge has fallen into the trap of *non sequitor*, where what is drawn as a conclusion simply does not follow from the reasons offered, or that of inconsistency, where two things he has tried to say are

36 *Alcock v Chief Constable of South Yorkshire* [1992] 1 AC 310 CA at 379.

37 [1993] Fam 32 per Sir Stephen Brown P at 38.

incompatible. To make either criticism, you must be able to show the precise respect in which the judge's argument lacks cogency. The judge may have failed to draw the conclusions that the evidence or principles imply: the criticism derives not from poor evidence but from reasoning poorly from good grounds, and in that sense the judgment can also be impeached as being uninformed.

In *The Miraflores and The Abadesa*,[38] a shipping case involving a collision, Winn LJ in the Court of Appeal found that he could not support the trial judge's approach, which he considered illogical:

> "In the incident which gave rise to this action there were two events, separate in space and time, though not widely separate in either of those elements. The collision between the Abadesa and the Miraflores was one of those events; the other, partially but not inevitably consequential upon it, was the grounding of the George Livanos. Each event was the subject of a separate action: Folio 218 in respect of the grounding, and Folio 228 in respect of the collision. Those actions were heard together. Of the two events, the earlier in point of time, the collision, was far and away the more serious, and it was in every respect natural that Hewson J. should have applied his mind first to determining the respective proportions of fault for that collision to be attributed to the two ships involved in it. He made such a determination, and assessed the Abadesa as two-thirds to blame and the Miraflores as one-third to blame. That was an assessment of fault in respect of the collision."

He then turned to a consideration of the causes or faults which produced the grounding of the George Livanos. He held that the George Livanos had herself been 50 per cent to blame for going aground, and had to that extent been the author of her own misfortune and damage. He expressed that determination thus:

> "In action Folio 218 I propose to treat the negligence leading to the collision . . . as one unit, and the negligence of the George Livanos as another.'
>
> It seems to me that, in so determining, Hewson J. was adopting a mental process of quasi-personification of the collision itself, and that what he was saying when he declared the George Livanos to be 50 per cent responsible for having gone aground was that half the cause of the grounding had been the collision and half the fault or faults of the George Livanos in respect of her navigation preceding the grounding. He said: 'In action Folio 218 I find it impossible to distinguish between the degrees of fault between the two units.' Save in so far as one of those units comprised two ships and the other only one, he did not anywhere in his judgment distinguish, in respect specifically of the grounding, the respective faults of the three individual ships involved.
>
> With the utmost respect to Hewson J. which I sincerely entertain for any view of his, I cannot help thinking that in this respect he fell into a logical fallacy. Since the collision was part of the causation of the grounding, the whole of the responsibility for that consequence of the collision, as

38 [1966] P 18 at 35 *et seq.*

> well as for the collision, has to be attributed to the respective vessels by whose fault the collision and that consequence of it were caused. As I see it, Hewson J. did not apportion at all one-half of the responsibility for producing the grounding. It having already been determined that the responsibility for producing the collision rested as to 66 2/3 per cent upon the Abadesa, and to 33 1/3 per cent upon the Miraflores, the reasoning might properly proceed on one or other of two parallel lines: either (1) the 50 per cent residue over and above the fault of the George Livanos for the occurrence of the grounding, that is, 50 per cent of the responsibility for that event, should be distributed equally upon each of the other two vessels so as to add 25 per cent of responsibility for the grounding and the damage caused thereby to the respective shares of responsibility for the collision; or (2) the share of the same 50 per cent responsibility for the grounding might be attributed to the Abadesa and the Miraflores in the same proportions precisely as those fixed in respect of the collision, so as to produce an assessment of 66 2/3 per cent of 50 per cent, that is, 33 1/3 per cent in respect of the grounding damage against the Abadesa, and, by parity of reasoning, 16 2/3 per cent (that is, 33 1/3 per cent of 50 per cent.) in respect of the grounding damage against the Miraflores.'
>
> Responsibility for an event does not terminate when the event occurs, but comprises liability for consequences flowing from the event. By such a method as I have suggested, it seems to me that there is achieved what is not achieved by Hewson J.'s approach: an assessment in respect of each ship of the overall responsibility for the occurrence of the double event of the collision and the partially consequential grounding. For the collision, of course, the George Livanos bore no responsibility. I venture to think that Hewson J. was led by the approach which he adopted to lay too much stress upon causation or causative potency and too little upon elements of blame to which due regard must be had; cf. *The British Aviator* et passim."

Once again, you are concerned with the respective defect only to the extent that major conclusions are affected by it, or perhaps by the cumulative effect of such defects. For our purposes a judgment may safely lack cogency in irrelevant respects. This class of criticism requires penetrative reading because the defects are usually well concealed.

Incompleteness

The basis of this critique is to say the judge has not solved all the problems he started with; or he has not made use of all the available material; or he did not see all the ramifications and implications; or he has failed to make all the distinctions relevant to his task. This might derive from his erroneous acceptance of facts which should be challenged, or it might be an incomplete analysis of thinking because it makes assumptions or fails to make assumptions. An example is to be found in the criticism of an arbitration award in *Drake Insurance Plc v Provident Insurance Plc* (CA):[39]

39 [2003] EWCA Civ 1834, [2004] QB 601 per Rix LJ at 621.

> "In my judgment, the judge was in error in concluding that there was no evidence to suggest that the no fault status of the prior accident would have emerged. Until 7 February 1997 Provident had said nothing to suggest that the disclosure of the fault accident had anything to do with its claim to avoid the policy. When, however, the connection with the status of that accident was first made in Mr Shaw's letter of that date, Dr Singh's next communication with Provident, his letter to the chief executive dated 5 March 1997, straightway pointed out that the accident had been a no fault one. It was the point he made in his first numbered paragraph, after the words: 'Mr Shaw did not mention in our telephone conversation any of the other points raised in his letter dated 6 February 1997, if he had I certainly would have corrected his misunderstandings . . .'
>
> 61. Dr Singh kept that point well in view, for instance in his letter in reply to the arbitrator. It was a great pity that in his award the arbitrator paid no attention whatsoever to this factor."

The Structured Critique

Make a list outlining all the problems which the judge is trying to solve. The last step of interpretation is to know which of these problems the judge solved and which he did not.

Assess, in respect of those problems he failed to solve, whether these impact on your client's position as a whole. If so, identify the basis of the omission in respect of each relevant fact or consequence omitted.

If not (or in addition), consider in respect of the problems which the judge did solve, how satisfactory the solutions are.

Identify those solutions which are to be the subject of complaint, classifying them as uninformed, misinformed or illogical.

Beyond the idea of preparing to criticise the judgment below fairly it is as well to consider circumstances where the judge was driven to make findings where the claim turned on the acceptance of expert evidence. If that is so the expert is likely to feature in the mediation. The ambit of using an expert in mediation generally has been discussed in *Effective Mediation Advocacy.*[40] But at this point it becomes necessary to consider how the judge dealt with the experts in the trial below.

The Judge and the Expert

Judges are called upon daily to determine disputes whose subjects may be scientific, technological or highly specialised so far as a particular trade, profession or industry is concerned. These may require an explanation of some or all of the material trade or technical jargon, methodology, professional standards, custom and practice, and both national and internationally recognised norms and models. Often the issue centres upon what is the relevant professional standard or trade practice, and whether liability occurs because a defendant has departed from such a standard or usage. Valuation

40 *Ibid.* p. 110.

may be an issue going to liability as well as quantum.

Where such matters are outside the experience or knowledge of the court, evidence of expert opinion in connection with the material issues will be called on if it will assist the judge in his decision-making process. There are three fundamentals of which we occasionally lose sight:

- The expert is *not* the judge and does not perform his function.
- Although based on recognised qualification and experience, ultimately expert evidence is only opinion.
- Like any other evidence that is received, the judge is free to reject it.

The judge should not be in awe of an expert and should try and treat such evidence with as much measured detachment as he would any other. Making allowances for the inherent respect due to expertise, experience and authority, the judge should nonetheless deal with weight and materiality with great care. In assessing the regard he has had to an expert when delivering judgment, you will wish to analyse whether the judge has ascertained:

- the relevance of the expert's qualifications to the facts in issue;
- the relevance of the expert's experience to the facts in issue;[41]
- whether the evidence has been given with true impartiality and lack of partisanship; if there is a dispute between experts of similar relevant standing, whether it is a 'genuine' or 'partisan' conflict;[42]
- whether the evidence has been of primary assistance to the court, or whether it is being used to corroborate evidence of fact or assertions of method;
- the true weight that should properly be attached to it.

Essentially, the judge should have asked the questions:

Is the expert neutral?

Is the expert reliable?

Is the expert representative?

Is the expert's evidence relevant and material?

The area in which judges meet most criticism concerning experts is in case management. Part 35 of the Civil Procedure Rules 1998 was intended to reduce the number of experts and have those appointed come to a consensus. It was

41 *National Justice Compania Naviera SA v Prudential Assurance Co Ltd ('The Ikarian Reefer')* [1995] 1 Lloyd's Rep 455 CA per Stuart-Smith LJ at 496, 497.

42 That is, whether there has been strict compliance with both CPR 35 and the spirit behind it.

also designed to reduce the risk of bias by requiring experts to certify their understanding of their overriding duty to the court. In assessing the outcome of any case involving experts, you will wish to examine how the judge's case management impacted on expert evidence, particularly in terms of the four criteria referred to above, and even more so when evidence of expert opinion was taken from a single joint appointee. Certainly, the conduct of experts can now be the subject of almost as much examination as the substance of what they have said.[43]

For ease of reference, judges like experts to provide them with a norm or constant against which they can measure the conduct of the defendant. This enables them to both rationalise and simplify their decision-making. However, although produced for the assistance of the court, expert evidence is not always designed or shaped for the contingencies of litigation, particularly in areas of science, technology and medicine. Here, and in other areas where new developments and continuing research may challenge existing benchmarks of expert opinion, the idea of a normal standard tends to be idealised by the courts. There is a presumption that research results are open and accessible, which is often not the case, and that scientific or technical knowledge is shared communally with all working for the common good, and thus that each expert has access to the same material, which is a hypothesis that deserves close scrutiny, since this is a somewhat naïve approach. Experts may be in competition with each other, particularly in a narrow field. They will wish to protect research work. They may have personal, cultural, financial or professional reasons for attaining primacy through presenting or publishing an opinion based on incomplete, partial or under-theorised results. This may be unknown to the client as well as the courts.

The judge has to determine whether the witness is providing evidence of expert opinion which is representative of the norm, or whether his evidence is novel and maverick, or in some other way only recognised by a small minority in the relevant scientific or technical community. The evidence may have been taken out of context; it may have been drawn from abstract statements, or statements only relevant where certain background assumptions, facts and interpretations are vital. As 'novel' evidence it may not altogether be accepted by the wider scientific community, or, at a slightly lower level, there may not exist anything approximating to universal support among, for example, scientists for a particular interpretation.

There has to be general acceptance of a scientific or medical principle for it to be admitted into evidence in the United States. In Australia[44] and England,[45] courts have been willing to admit evidence purportedly accepted by a

43 See e.g. *Selman v Vijay Construction (UK) Ltd* [2003] EWHC TCC 1100, HH Judge Thornton QC.

44 *R v Gilmore* [1977] 2 NSWLR 935 at 939–941; *Runjanjic and Kontinen v The Queen* (1991) 56 SASR 114, 119; *R v Rose* (1993) A Crim R 1, 9; *R v J* (1994) 75 A Crim R 522, 535–6; *R v Jarrett* (1994) 62 SASR 443.

45 *Maynard v West Midlands Regional Health Authority* [1984] 1 WLR 634 at 639; *Bolitho v City and Hackney Health Authority* [1998] AC 232, 238–239, 241–242.

minority in a particular field, if it comes within the compass of a 'recognised body of opinion'.

The judge, then, has to fall back on the analytical and reasoning skills he applies to other categories of evidence, namely assessing materiality, reliability and weight, in viewing the expert. He may wish to consider such matters as:

- Are the norms used by the experts consistent or inconsistent with each other or with any other published measured standards?
- What is the degree of certainty being espoused?
- Have any boundaries been crossed between different professional activities?
- What impression is given by the demeanour and authority of the expert?
- Is the expert being dogmatic or flexible in his opinion?
- Notwithstanding that the expert has all relevant professional information, has he taken in the facts of the case adequately?

Finally, one of the judge's basic tasks is to choose between experts of differing opinion. He must be able to show that he has a reasoned basis for his preference: the factors by which he has drawn a distinction may be categorised as:

(a) what the witnesses have actually said;

(b) the extent to which what they have said is lent authority by their respective qualifications and experience;

(c) the relationship between their respective qualification and experience and the task in hand;

(d) where the weight of the evidence in terms of general principle lies, i.e. the novelty of the propositions being advanced, and the relative support of the technical or scientific community to which the expert is attached to their norm or model.

Preparing for Appellate Mediation Schemes

When you come to structure appellate argument as a negotiating tool you will obviously apply general principles of power imbalance in the mediation by analysing and leveraging the decision of the Court below. This may be limited to considering

- The obviously wrong judgment
- A degree of uncertainty created by permission to appeal from the Court below

- Valuing the prospects of success for negotiating purposes
- Accepting that new law may be necessary and calculating the value of precedent

Almost inevitably you will have to apply evaluative approaches to measure the value of the first instance judgment. Your analysis of the Court below's decision making will include:

- The mechanics of fact finding – how the judge went about findings of fact, to include
- Receiving and weighing evidence, in terms of relative value
- The extent to which the judge relied upon impression or inference
- The adequacy or paucity of materials available to the judge
- Discretion – its exercise and restriction
- Authority and jurisdiction - the power to make decisions
- Transparency

Beyond that, preparation for the mediation will centre on you and the client finding true alternatives to the litigation/judgment below. This will be a search for value and is likely also to be a classic expansion of the pie. It may involve wider stakeholders, probably non-parties to the existing claim, and call for mixed motive negotiation.

One of the advantages of the present judgment is the existing value of the Respondent's interest is known. If there was any doubt before, or a potential range of values, these have been removed by the judge's findings. This value operates in the same way as an anchor, and any new negotiation will gravitate towards that figure. The idea that mediation as managed negotiation is a means of advanced risk analysis, where both parties are effectively buying out risk, to a greater or smaller degree of satisfaction, is distorted by the starting point.

In addition there are significant disadvantages – beyond moving into evaluation – in that parties are drawn to a retrospective rather than prospective view, the latter being a hallmark of the mediation process. Nor does there appear to be any room for using the value of potential public vindication as a negotiating proposition, since any such value has been exhausted. If the trial was publicised, the value in confidentiality has also, to a large extent, been dissipated.

The Royal Courts of Justice Annual Tables[46] shows an upward trend in appeals allowed after full hearing as a percentage of disposals:

2017 38.73%;

2018 43.7%;

2019 45.32%;

2020 46.87%.

For the purpose of negotiated discounting it is possible to apply a broad statistical analysis. There are other pertinent factors – the time over which an appeal might keep the Respondent from the proceeds of the judgment; the costs of the exercise; the risk associated with such costs, and whether the costs below will become at large again; the costs of a potential retrial if that is either the intended or directed result.

There is much to prepare for, and much to consider, and the successful mediation advocate will not approach these matters lightly.

---

46 2020 edition; see also *Civil Justice Statistics Quarterly and Appellate Court Statistics* HMSO.

Chapter 6
International Mediation

Preparing for and Engaging in Cross-border, Multi-national and Cross-cultural work

Introduction

Since 2009 I have been fortunate enough to experience working in mediation in over 20 jurisdictions, including countries within Africa, the Arabian Gulf, South-East Asia and the Far East, the Sub-Continent, and the European Union. Outside the United Kingdom I have mediation practices in Turkey, Hong Kong SAR, India, Thailand, Nepal and Nigeria – quite an eclectic mix.

Mediating in a cross-border or multi-national dispute adds a completely new dimension to what you are doing. For me it adds a layer of preparation which takes in the various considerations I want to write about: foreign mediation practice and procedure; jurisdictional and linguistic issues; dealing with foreign and multi-jurisdictional lawyers; option generation, settlement enforcement and workability; cultural barriers to negotiation and how to recognise and overcome them.

I also want to focus on mediating in the English language with non-native speakers and the particular challenges this brings both to advocate, client and the mediator.

One of the core considerations in non-UK work is mediator selection due to the different scope of the mediator's work. Building a rapport in cross-border mediation is very different from doing that in a domestic situation, simply because one of the parties is likely to be from the mediator's jurisdiction and the other party will not be. Therefore, for the mediator there is much greater effort required to remove any perception of bias, and much more time and effort to consume in engaging the advocates before the mediation starts, which is likely also to occur with mediators operating online from another country. It may be that co-mediation with mediators from each party's jurisdiction is required, or a single mediator from neither of their jurisdictions, which may present its own difficulties in language and culture.

Why should the mediation advocate care about the need for additional preparation by the mediator? One of the difficulties in cross-cultural work is finding a settlement that is certain and durable, that is lawful and workable in both jurisdictions, and one that isn't going to fall apart the moment a party gets on an aeroplane and starts thinking on the flight back about what happened during the course of the mediation. Durability is one of the reasons why, as an advocate, you take a slightly different approach in deciding where to start when preparing your mediation.

Practitioners will need to have an appreciation of quite a number of different factors that may be extremely pertinent to the conduct of the mediation. These include the likelihood of procedural collaboration from the other party or parties if their background in mediation is different from yours, workable option generation, and a mutually acceptable outcome. There may be mediation practice and procedural issues, jurisdictional, linguistic, socio-cultural, trust, religious, political, historic and societal concerns involving tribal influence, and family or political hierarchies and custom. In addition, information may be needed about relevant local business practices, governance and structures, monetary, and value systems.

It is necessary also to return to the basic principles of mediation practice in which the mediator has to demonstrate a regard for all the participants, including the practitioner, and not merely the parties which in some jurisdictions may be challenging. The mediator must engage with everybody in the room since it is quite likely that each person or entity they represent has a good reason for being there, and their reasons may be very different.

Problematically, a mediator from another jurisdiction may see lawyers foreign to them as an impediment to his or her work, a barrier to settlement, and an obstacle which prevents him or her building a rapport directly with their clients, who may be working in a second or even a third language.

Where external lawyers are involved, most mediators do not get access to the clients until the day of the mediation itself. Under those circumstances there is a limit to what the mediator can do beforehand to engage the parties, and the building of rapport comes in two separate stages: first, with the lawyer, and second with the client. These approaches by the mediator are going to be noticeably, though subtly, different as between these stages.

Legal issues apart, for the mediator, and therefore for the mediation advocate, what is important are those factors which are likely to influence the outcome of the process and the mediator/advocate/party relationship as it develops. The challenge is how to relate to and afterwards harness things which come from different fields – from sociology, from anthropology, from technical professional work. The mediator must try to bring these together and apply them in the course of the work being undertaken with people from different cultures, different nations, different languages and different commercial experience sitting in the room.

The advocate needs to engage with, but not rely on, the mediator. It may not always be possible to attune to the linguistic or cultural nuances of those with whom the practitioner is having a conversation, but that they exist must be known and accepted. The path to settlement is likely to require a moderation of personal values, and the sense of 'being right.' An early manifestation of from where the outcome may originate is whether the client sees the settlement as a reflection of his 'being right' in the dispute, or rather wishes to secure an outcome that makes him 'better off'.

Doing international work means bumping up against jurisdictional and cultural issues. That is inevitable. There may also be an unspoken but tangible political dimension which heavily underpins what it is possible to do in a place, and who practitioners may act for. The risk profile to your client may become elevated, whether the advocate likes it or not, consequent upon the prevailing political climate. For that very reason there may be an opportunity to persuade the reluctant client to get out of the local civil justice system and into mediation.

This is as much part of risk analysis for your client as any other appraisal of the case. It may concern whether a settlement is enforceable, whether money or assets can be taken out of the country in which you are mediating, whether your client may own property there as a foreigner, or what a settlement in a 'soft' currency will amount to.

With that introduction I want to start by examining three themes:

- Foreign mediation practice and procedure.
- Jurisdictional aspect of cross-border mediation.
- The impact of culture and language, and, taking the two together, considering certain aspects of the mediation process that are affected by this.

1. Foreign mediation practice and procedure

Significant developments in mediation and the recognition of the importance of ADR generally has been a feature of legal systems across the world since the global pandemic. The coming into force of new Mediation Acts in India[1] and Turkey,[2] and the growing number of signatories[3] and ratifiers[4] of the Singapore Convention on Mediation 2019 suggest that you need to know much more about local practice and procedure in any country other than your own where you intend your client to mediate.[5]

Increasingly mediation is seeing greater regulation, supervision and mandate by the courts in many jurisdictions. Practitioners must understand the relationship between the courts and mediation in the jurisdiction in

1 The Mediation Act 2023

2 Mediation Laws No. 6100 and 6325, which entered into force in 2013; followed by Article 5/A to the Commercial Code No. 6102 on 06.12.2018 with Article 20 of Law No. 7155. With this regulation, in commercial cases, receivables and compensation claims, the subject matter of which is money, must first be applied to the mediator. Parallel to the regulation on mediation as a condition of litigation in the Labour Courts Law, mediation as a condition of litigation is regulated in the Commercial Code as a mandatory remedy that must be taken before the related lawsuits are filed. In addition to these regulations, Article 73/A of the Law No. 6502 on the Protection of Consumers introduces the obligation to apply to a mediator for disputes before the consumer courts, coming into force in 2020.

3 57 countries at the time of writing

4 14 countries at the time of writing

5 I am grateful to Manon and Fred Schonewille for kind permission to use the list of questions on the fly cover of their book *The Variegated Landscape of Mediation* eleven 2014 as the basic structure of the following passage.

question: is mediation voluntary or mandatory? If it is court referred, what are the implications for the outcome and for confidentiality? What sanctions operate either by law or by the courts if mediation is not tried in good faith? Is mediation incentivised in any way? Is the presence of outside counsel during mediation sessions for representation permissible, mandatory or merely desirable?

Will the courts give effect to contractual mediation clauses and stay proceedings? Are either the fact or contents of the mediation admissible in court?

If mediation operates as an established procedure, are the duties of the mediator prescribed by law? Is there any flexibility in the style of the mediator according to the parties' agreement – may he or she offer a non-binding or binding opinion? Is the predominant style of mediation facilitative, evaluative, transformative or another variant? Does that depend on whether the dispute would otherwise be founded on commercial law, or other specialised civil process?

Is the predominant mediation procedure for the entire process to be in joint session/s, or only caucusing, or a flexible series of meetings according to the management of the mediator and/or the wishes of the parties? Is online mediation permissible and are there rules appertaining?

Are civil/commercial mediators accredited, registered, regulated or certified by the Ministry of Justice, another governmental agency or NGO, the local Bar or Law Society, internationally recognised accrediting bodies, or by private concerns? Is there a minimum number of hours of entry-level training, followed by mandatory continuing professional development? Is accreditation through a formal set of rules, written examination or through performance-based assessment? Are the assessment criteria set by public regulation or by the market? Is mediator accreditation in either domestic or cross-border work confined to lawyers, and if so, of a certain seniority or status?

Are there specific requirements for mediators who wish to engage in cross-border work?

Are there similar requirements for recognition or accreditation as a mediation advocate?

Does the particular jurisdiction subscribe to EU Directives on mediation incorporated into domestic law for national or international work, or the EU Code of Conduct for Mediators? Is it a signatory to the Singapore Convention on Mediation 2019, and if so, what is its ratification status?

How are mediation service provider bodies formed and governed? Do they have different legal forms? Are they subject to public regulation or qualification? Can individual mediators practice independently?

How is the mediator fee determined? Can the mediator contract freely or is there some form of public regulation fixing a fee scale? What is the average fee rate in commercial or cross-border cases? Is that a fee per hour, or is the fee based on minimum work to be provided – preparation and reading in, pre-mediation conferencing, the mediation day/s.

Is there public financing available for the parties in mediation? Is there legal aid available, or are mediator fees covered by insurance schemes? If the mediation is court mandated or directed are the fees subsidised by the civil justice process?

What is the relationship – if any – between the judges and the civil justice process and mediation? Is court-directed mediation regarded as part of civil justice or independent of it? Is there state resistance or lawyer/judicial resistance to ADR? How tangible is local judicial support for the concept of mediation? Is there real movement towards normalising mediation or is the support mere lip service to get cases out of the courts but with no resources or infrastructure provided?

What substantive law issues may be of concern in this jurisdiction: for example, does the mediation impact on time running for the purpose of limitation or prescription? How are settlements obtained by mediation enforced: as a contract which replaces the original dispute or an instrument capable of being registered as a court judgment; if the latter, is it automatically enforceable, or by express agreement between the parties, or enforceable only in limited circumstances as defined by public regulation?

Is the confidentiality of the mediation process regulated by law? Is there a specific mediation privilege vested in the mediator? What is the regime in countries that do not recognise 'without prejudice' negotiations? Is the mediator exempted in any case from being compelled to give evidence as a witness of what took place in the mediation?

Is mediator and/or mediation advocacy a recognised component of the core curriculum of legal education?

Once this information is compiled there will undoubtedly be variation. If you have the opportunity to select the jurisdiction in which the mediation will be held there will be factors that significantly influence your decision, and these will most likely be from among the answers to these questions.

The information will also give you an understanding of the mediation hinterland from where the mediator, and potentially opposing counsel, originates and the predominant practice with which he or she will be familiar. Compare and contrast that with your own, and you will see where potential advantages and difficulties may lie.

2. Jurisdictional aspects of cross-border mediation

Lawyer mediators, particularly in jurisdictions where mediation is regulated and mediators are restricted to being qualified lawyers of a certain seniority, have the advantage of calling upon the fraternity or confraternity of lawyers which exists irrespective of jurisdiction because lawyers anywhere in the world tend to gravitate towards each other, sharing professional and ethical norms. The mediation advocate will already have the ability to build rapport with the mediator on a professional level. This is particularly true of common lawyers who share a legal heritage from the English-speaking nations.

Despite reaching back into prehistory in the search for indigenous roots of mediation and ADR processes, particularly in Asia and the sub-continent, in its modern form of development the Pacific Rim countries were principally responsible for the revival and re-establishment of mediation, the majority being from the common law jurisdictions of the United States, Canada, Australia, New Zealand, Hong Kong, Malaysia and Singapore. Practitioners were trained and familiar with the adversarial system and tried to adapt their style as advocates to what they thought was required of them to defend the interests of their clients in mediation. Practitioners from civil law systems, on the other hand, may feel that the role of the mediator is essentially inquisitorial, and orthodox advocacy – certainly in the sense of being adversarial - has no real place.

So perhaps the first question to ask is from what kind of jurisdiction does the dispute of the parties emerge – Common Law or Civil Law. In addition, for a small number of countries, particularly, but not exclusively in the Islamic world, jurisdiction may derive from a religious law system. Beyond Shariah, the dispute may be governed by the parties' submission to the Halakah or Canon (ecclesiastical) law. The dispute may be drawn from a hybrid-based jurisdiction.

So, from where do the parties come? This should tell the mediator instinctively and automatically something about the lawyers coming from such a background. Are they trained as civil or common lawyers? In civil law jurisdictions codified law is very accessible. It is easy to establish what the basic law is, although the interpretation by different courts may vary in the absence of a system of precedent and with courts of similar hierarchy having competing views of the same problem within a broad framework. A mediator might reasonably be expected to gain access to the local civil code and quickly develop a sufficient bare bones understanding of the appropriate legal issues in that jurisdiction. However, the problem is that in civil law countries the law is inflexible and difficult to change since it can generally only be amended or removed by the legislature, and therefore may be unresponsive to the present and immediate needs of the parties to the matter in hand, which has to be applied by civil law courts in a semi-rigid way. And that is going to be reflected in the thinking processes of the lawyer appearing for the party that comes from a civil law jurisdiction.

Of course this is a generalization, which is not advisable, but you have to start somewhere.

If there is a common law party representative or mediation advocate then the great thing about the common law is its flexibility. What that means is the advocate is almost inevitably going to be a problem solver, since their work requires them to be creative, imaginative and to make full use of the law available to them in a very flexible way. This is because their experience is of common law judges who are instinctively concerned to deliver immediate practical justice to the parties then in front of them. The downside is, of course, for all common law jurisdictions, because the law is in a state of organic growth and changes every day senior courts opine, citizens need a lawyer to tell them what the law is. If the mediator is dealing with a dispute from a common law jurisdiction other than his or her own, he will have to rely on the mediation advocate to tell him what the law is there, should the problem descend to an orthodox legal analysis which is relevant in the mediation.

Thus, for different reasons, but which both go to outcome, in the two major systems of civil jurisprudence, lawyers working in contentious business are driven to measure and manage their client's risk of losing a case in a binary system where the odds are generally stacked against either party being completely successful to the extent of satisfying a traditional cost benefit analysis. The exceptions are disputes of such magnitude that neither cost nor delay are of much significance to the value of the outcome.

But there is more to that when considering matters of jurisdiction.

First is the question of the enforceability of the mediation agreement, and of the settlement agreement, and of the process in the middle. So for a mediator working creatively, there are some countries where the legal system does not admit any form of 'without prejudice' communication kept from the court. How then to mediate within a strictly confidential process that usually operates within two familiar levels of confidentiality, the one covering the entirety of the mediation and the other, the particular requirements of the private caucus?

Usually, the parties are given this double layer of protection, supported by the courts, which gives them the confidence to explain their interests and concerns, and to make concessions in the hope of securing something of value in return, this confidence being based on their absence of fear that anything said during the course of the mediation can be used by the other side and reported to the court.

When faced with this problem the mediator has to find an answer quickly that will meet the needs of a concerned party. One answer is to use hypothesis – mediating on the basis almost of extreme hypothesis, because here there are no offers made between the parties. Everything that passes between them is passes on the basis of hypothesis – e.g. the mediator will say, "this is not an offer, and you must understand that: but were it to be an offer, how would you respond?" It becomes a sort of dance, but that may be the best the mediator can do under the circumstances.

There may be authority issues which vary according to jurisdiction. The mediator does not want to fall into the trap of getting the parties to apparent agreement which then requires ratification. If ratification falls down, one party or the other may run off to the local courts in order to demonstrate their contention that they have been offered a sum of money as proof of the fact that they are owed more. This is dealt with in more detail below.

These two are merely examples of why you need to be aware of how the jurisdiction of both parties will operate firstly on the agreement to mediate but more importantly on the enforceability of the mediation settlement.

The jurisdictions of the world that allow mediation are also divided between those who recognise the settlement as immediately enforceable and registrable with the court as if it were a judgment, akin to an arbitral award, and those where the settlement is simply an enforceable contract which replaces the subject matter of the dispute, and where enforcement follows breach of that agreement. In cross-border mediation the impact of the Singapore convention has yet to be felt, with the limited number of ratifying states growing very slowly. But that will change over time. It should be remembered that both domestic legislation[6] and caveats in the Convention itself[7] will also limit its scope.

The next jurisdictional issue is the impact of regulation on the mediator. If the lawyers come from either a regulatory or non-regulatory background that will colour their expectations of the proficiency of the chosen mediator, the process he or she may adopt, and their own view of what is or is not appropriate for the mediator to do, particularly during the negotiation phase. It may also impact their view of the context of mediation within existing or intended litigation, should the mediation fail to bring about settlement. It may have an effect on the structure of the mediation agreement because a regulatory framework is likely to introduce content which is required by at least one side as a matter of law.

Whether regulation either requires or precludes the mediator from having a role in the drafting of the settlement agreement is a matter that must be addressed. In unregulated jurisdictions, particularly where the parties are unrepresented, mediators tend to have no involvement in drafting the settlement agreement but may come under pressure from the parties to do so; they should resist this temptation because of the risk of making a mistake. At best they may assist unrepresented parties in identifying heads of agreement and advise them jointly to retain a lawyer to complete any formal drafting. However, in Turkey, Greece and Brazil the law requires that the agreement be settled by the mediator, and in these and other jurisdictions court-appointed mediators are required to sign the settlement agreement under their respective Mediation legislation.[8] Article 4(b)(i) and (ii) of the Singapore Convention requires the mediator's signature on the settlement agreement, or some form of certification by him or her that a mediation took place. Effectively this means the mediator accepts responsibility for the settlement being legal, workable, sufficiently certain and enforceable. That is one of the quid pro quos of it being mandatory for the mediator to be a lawyer, and is a manifestation of the mediator's independence, that he or she will be responsible for drafting the settlement.

Thus neither the mediator nor mediation advocates should be blind to the jurisdictional issues that arise in considering from where a party comes. At the very least the mediator needs to ask the lawyers whether they are coming from a jurisdiction where mediation is regulated and what those regulations mean for the mediator's job.

---

6 For example ss 27,28 Indian Mediation Act 2023

7 See Article 8

8 In Germany under art 6(2) Mediationsgesecht the mediator can draft the settlement agreement with the consent of the parties.

Finally, in terms of jurisdiction, one must revert to considering authority to settle. This can be a real issue for mediators, particularly when one side is away from 'home' and may need to revert there for instructions and ratification. It may fit into an aspect of the cultural considerations of the parties. The problem arises when the mediator has been assured of sufficient authority, either by the signing of the mediation agreement which contains a relevant provision, or by the express assurance of a lawyer or party who is present, and it later emerges that the authority to settle is either limited or worse still, illusory.

The difficulty is plainly that where the parties appear to come to terms, the settlement must be ratified by those in authority elsewhere who were not present at the mediation and may have concerns about how the settlement came about. They may value the settlement differently from their representatives or lawyers. They may be adversely influenced by others who were not there. That is not necessarily an international or cross-border problem, since the same issue does occur in domestic mediation, probably more commonly that we would like to admit, but it may be a reflection of a culture in which it is acceptable to indicate the existence of authority to the mediator only to reveal limitations on that authority later in the process. In international work there is a logistical element that overlays this problem: how long is it going to take to obtain ratification, or to get the appropriate signature on the settlement agreement?

There are some other core issues: who is going to do the ratifying? What effect is that going to have on the other party? Is there a cultural perspective that is relevant? How this is going to be seen may be very significant. In some cultures it may be perceived as an act of betrayal, and the mediator may have to spend a lot of time explaining that the settlement remains in place.

So, a principal concern is where does authority lie? In cross-border work if the mediator is dealing with in-house or external counsel with whom he is unfamiliar, it must be known whether authority lies with the lawyers – which is a helpful and good starting point – but if it doesn't lie with the lawyers does it lie with the parties, with some other participant, such as an insurer or third party funder, or does it lie completely outside the room, requiring ratification by a treasury committee, finance officer, the head of a family or clan, by a tribal elder, by the Sheikh, or the ruling family?

It may be that ratification in certain places will pass up a decision tree. Practitioners may be participating in a jurisdiction where commercial activity may be at the whim of a ruling family or a political elite, where you are really not sure of the nature of the authority the other party brings to the table. While it is difficult to prepare for, practitioners should not allow themselves to be surprised by an event that occurs at mediation, and need to warn their client accordingly; although, as the party to the commercial activity which provides the background to the dispute, he is probably already aware. In cross-border work in particular always expect the unexpected unless there is the comfort of a familiar approach borne from the experience of dealing with a particular sector in a particular jurisdiction.

3. The impact of culture and language

My fellow mediator Janeen Achtar tells me, "I like the word 'Shuohe' which means 'speaking peace', the term the Chinese use to mean "to mediate." Indeed in the Chinese culture, bargaining and mediation play a crucial role in dispute resolution as they perceive that these two procedures as more capable of reducing the animosity between the disputants. This is similar to the Japanese culture where the emphasis on harmony results in 'a strong expectation that a dispute shall not and will not arise, even when one does, it shall be solved by mutual understanding.' These cultural proclivities reflect the fact that in these cultures relationship values are significant – they would prefer to trust people they already know more than the qualifications of strangers. That is something to think about. It also means that securing an apology from a party of these two cultures will be both difficult and a concession of real substance.

Identifying cultural proclivity feeds into how practitioners prepare and what they are likely to face. In the same way that one can divide up the world's jurisdictions into common law, civil law and religious based systems, which may cover every country in the world except perhaps North Korea and possibly Cuba, so anthropologists through research divide up most nations into one of three different kinds of culture, and I know that people may be familiar with the media driven stereotype of 'face' culture.

In mediation some of the leading writers[9] in the field are not lawyers, but are anthropologists.

There are three prototypes of culture – dignity, face and honour. These stem apparently from two factors in particular over the course of prehistory – population density and type of economy. Recognising whether you are engaging with a dignity, face or honour culture may help mediators in their preparation, and advocates to understand their own client's and that of the other side's thinking, and certainly during the course of the negotiation phase of the process may help mediators understand what is going to move somebody from a particular type of cultural background.

Dignity cultures value their independence and they are reasonably trustful at the outset. They stem from societies built on an agrarian economy with a low population density. And these developed into individual rather than collective efforts in societal organization so they prize independence, and do not particularly wish to rely upon other people. In mediation participants from dignity cultures tend to show they will meet conflict rationally and directly and will avoid strong emotional reactions, because in most dignity cultures they are supported by an effective system of law and strong economic markets. And they therefore tend to trust people. I'm talking about the USA, Canada, northern Europe – societies with a strong economic hinterland which promote and rewards individual effort, governed by the rule of law with a mature civil justice system.

9 See *Dispute Processing* Simon Roberts and Michael Palmer and in his latest book *Possible* William Ury describes himself as an anthropologist.

People from this background prefer a collaborative approach to negotiation, and what that means is they tend to explore interests and priorities by engaging in questions and evaluating answers. The mediator will therefore know that the starting point for Americans, Canadians and north Europeans is to obtain information by asking questions of the other side and analysing the answers they receive together with the mediator, whom they will expect to engage in reality testing and carry further questions to the other party. They will expect all this to be done before even considering making an offer to open the negotiation phase. They want offers to be contextualized, and to be confident that when offers are exchanged they are based on the information they have already received.

By way of contrast 'face' cultures, familiarly east Asian societies, particularly China and Japan, sprang up in agricultural regions with rapid expansion in population. Organized food production was required and that led to collectivism facilitated by cooperation and strong central government. Face cultures have a reputation for collective social responsibility, great respect for elders and traditions, and they encourage people as a (cultural) social norm to save face and protect harmony by avoiding direct confrontation, trying to suppress negative emotions, and deferring to authority.

In mediation this manifests itself in such parties taking a much more indirect approach to communication, stemming from a lack of trust. They are less open and have much less interest in probing the other side through questions and answers. By contrast this is likely to manifest itself by an early exchange of offers, since the development of the necessary information comes at the offer/negotiation phase and not the earlier exploration phase.

So members of a face-based society use offers to derive the information from which to justify their acceptance or rejection. This leads to a very conservative and economic linguistic approach. The language used is likely to be non-confrontational, but it carries a sub-text, and it is the sub-text that is important for the mediator and advocate to know; and, of course, the mediator will have to convey the sub-text to the lawyer on the other side from another culture, who may be *listening* to the language but not *hearing* the message.

An offer is likely to be accompanied by an underlying message which is not apparent on its face. It is important for the mediator to correctly interpret that message and be able to convey it to a party from another culture, usually by means of reframing where appropriate. There is an obvious risk that in reframing the mediator may create an impression in the mind of the lawyer that this is merely a matter of semantics (particularly in Western culture). It is extremely difficult to reframe and at the same time cross a cultural divide, so not only is the mediator advancing a new perspective from which the subject matter can be viewed, as he would for a domestic mediation, he must find new language with which to express the meaning intended by the conveying party.

For example, a Japanese rebuttal of an offer: the party tells the mediator 'this is difficult'. That is all that is said. In fact they are saying 'no' and also 'we will not negotiate further on this point'. A party from a dignity culture will not understand that being told 'this is difficult' is an end of the discussion on that point. They will attempt to keep the conversation going on that issue by modifying their position or linking it to another item of the agenda, but their Japanese counterpart will not be receptive because mentally he has moved on and might become irked by the failure of the other party to recognize that and do so himself. I understand that the Japanese have 15 words for avoiding saying 'no' directly yet politely disagreeing. There is an emphasis on 'maybe', 'perhaps', 'not correct', 'I'm afraid so', 'let me see', 'it's a little ...', 'I understand, but...', 'that's impossible' or more idiomatically 'that's not it'.

So here is the mediator as interpreter. While the mechanism of reframing is used in domestic mediation, the mediator/lawyers doing so in cross-cultural work have these added layers of difficulty. Where lawyers from a dignity culture may consider reframing a semantic exercise, using it in cross-cultural interpretation with a face culture lawyer gives an edge to what is happening: a mistake by the mediator could be very costly to the process, undermining trust in his or her competence generally, and specifically to convey the appropriate message at the right time. It might be enough to drive a party out of the process due to mistaken interpretation. The mediator may be treading a tightrope and the mediation advocate should recognize this, help be the interface between the mediator and the client, and where necessary speak to the mediator privately to support him or her through this difficulty.

The third cultural group is known as honour culture. This values strong ties and strong emotions. These are the peoples of the Middle East, North Africa, Latin America and parts of southern Europe. The anthropologists say that these were regions originally with low population density with economies based originally on the herding of animals. The cultural driver stems from the difficulties of defending herds from theft and poaching. The loss of a herd would bring destitution to a community. Psychological traits were developed to deter theft. Honour cultures projected an image of strength and robustness; reliance on family or relatively small communal groups; developing and being guided by a code of honour; and a people who take insults very seriously indeed. An insult is seen to be an attack on somebody's honour, and they are not prepared to suppress negative emotions. They are quick to take offence and to anger and will heat up a dispute more readily. They value the importance of revenge. However, for the mediator the obverse will be the importance of a genuine and appropriate apology and a restitutionary approach towards wrongdoing.

The danger in categorizing cultural groups is that the mediator and the lawyer may both fall into the trap of stereotyping participants in the process. In reality, recognizing a prototype is not necessarily going to be the key to unlocking cross-cultural difficulties, and should not be regarded as such. At best it may give practitioners a steer as to whether it is more important to spend a lot of time in the exploration phase or to move into more of an exploratory/offer phase leading to negotiation quite quickly during the course of the mediation. It may help with the viability of a successful opening plenary session, or whether it is likely that, stereotypically, parties will wish to give vent to anger and emotion.

In the mediation process where there are these different cultural aspects, it should be clear whether the mediator will make more progress by keeping the parties together, or by keeping them apart. Without overly generalizing, looking at these socio-cultural backgrounds provides some introductory guidance as to the participants and is something of an aid in how to prepare. It should be treated as a starting point which is better than nothing. Of course most modern societies, particularly post-industrial societies, will now have a blend of these prototypes as cities become more cosmopolitan than perhaps we would be prepared to admit. For example, and particularly in an election year, it is fun to note that London is now the sixth largest French city, with approximately 350,000 French residents. It is the 13th or 14th largest Polish city with 150,000 residents. It is the 67th largest German city with 136,000 residents. And so on, and so forth, with 270 nationalities speaking 300 languages and representing nearly 40% of the population.

And somebody from a prototypical culture may be completely different when you meet them, because they may have become imbued with societal influences drawn from a host community where they lived, including variations or modification of custom in transplanted communities that are reflective of the roots of members, but which are in fact based on false or idealized memory.

Anthropologists may also fail to take into account significant factors which impact on the way people behave, for example education in a host country that was unavailable in a homeland by reason of economic disadvantage or gender inequality, or the availability of a new shared experience or mentoring. The mediator must take this into account.

The mediator needs to understand the historical context of the dispute. Does it sit within a particular framework of interests, particularly interests that may be obscured? These may be governmental, societal, tribal, family, or religious. Is the framework formalized, or driven by a particular economic context or even an economic philosophy? Is one of the parties governmental, perhaps through an agency, and if so, is there a political or policy element? In such circumstances it is quite likely that policy will be more important than culture, although there may be elements of both.

It is important for the mediator to understand the societal context. What is the structure of the society from which the participants come? In particular, what is the role of hierarchies? For example, the structure of Japanese corporations is regarded as very rigid and hierarchical, which will be reflected in the approach of the participant to the other people in the room, where they are going to sit and, whether, and if so, what anybody is going to say by way of participation. This will have an impact right the way through the plenary session, the caucusing and the outcome. It is simply something for the mediator and opposing mediation advocates to be aware of all the time.

This kind of rigid hierarchy may give a formalization to the process which is inconsistent with a particular mediator's or advocate's normal way of working. The mediator may have been selected for a particular style or approach and may find that he or she is being forced to operate within constraints no one expected when hired. That suggests another selection criterion will be sufficient robustness to meet the situation without the process failing very near its beginning. It may be particularly disconcerting for the mediator who operates on a laissez-faire basis, allowing the parties to run the process and exercising a light touch. That may simply not be possible. The mediation advocate will have to alter his or her style to meet the occasion, since it is unlikely the corporate party on the other side of the table will alter their framework for the advocate.

It is also as well to remember that most western societies are liberal minded with regard to things such as dress, or at least accepted business dress, which may for example be seen differently in societies where there is a hierarchical approach to gender. Things may possibly have changed since the pandemic, but there are many examples of countries where it is perfectly apparent that the role of women is different from that of men as perceived by their society. You cannot equalize it as an outsider. The mediator will have to be made aware of what the roles will be if they are gender specific to the people in the room; whether women have a place at the table; or in extreme cases, whether there is a customary prohibition on speaking directly to women. Both mediator and the foreign or visiting mediation advocate have to find out about this in advance in case it presents a problem. This may extend to modes of address, or any address at all. It may happen in unexpected places. But however that may offend modern western sensibilities, in the context of what the mediation is trying to achieve, if that participant's society is comfortable with what they do and what they believe, both mediator and party representative from a different culture should accept the position and work on. Who are you to make a judgment, particularly if you are just coming in for a very short period, possibly as little as a day or two and then going away again?

Mediator Selection in International Work

I turn now to the concerns of mediation advocates faced with a cross-jurisdictional problem or the appearance of foreign lawyers with whom to engage. It probably goes without saying that if foreign lawyers are involved then foreign clients from jurisdictions other than your own will be involved in cross-border, multi-lingual or multi-cultural disputes. There is a wealth of material available on conflict of laws and choice of law. For the mediation advocate, questions arising from legal issues in jurisdictions other than your own, whether procedural or substantive, are fairly easy to research. There is nothing specialized about managing cross-border issues if it appertains to a matter of law.

In choosing a mediator we start by attaching the usual labels – facilitative, evaluative, normative, transformative, transitional – which we create. Some of the labels attach to process, some to the way mediators have been trained to a particular school of thought, but they are simply industry labels. Most basic entry-level training is designed to produce facilitative, non-judgmental mediators who may develop in their practice into more evaluative mediators, or at least apply evaluative strategies. There can be a distinction between what the industry wishes to provide, and what the market wants. There may even be a distinction between what the lawyer wants and what the client wants.

The lawyers, and invariably the clients, want guided robustness in commercial decision-making. If we scrap the labels we use, then it is best to focus on the role or nature of the mediator you wish to choose. Was the mediator chosen to be passive, or to be an activist? To be interventionist, or advisory? Has he or she been chosen to be robust with your own client as well as the other side? These descriptions are not being given in a vacuum. Operating in a cross-cultural context, the first question is how is the mediator going to be seen if acting in either a robust or a passive way? That is very much a matter of cultural perspective. It is like wearing sunglasses to which a different filter can be applied, looking at the same picture but with tinted strengths or colours that distort perception. Whatever the perception may be, the lawyer and or his or her client will view the mediator in a particular way. Cultural differences may magnify that perception – even unreasonably. Therefore, it is vital for the mediator's preparation to understand how he or she is going to be seen by the occupants of the room. An authority figure, commanding respect; a manager who is process driven; a guide with sufficient laissez-faire qualities to allow the parties to do as much as they can by themselves; a proactive, interventionist who can keep momentum going.

Let us presume the mediator has been appointed on the basis of reputation because he or she is the kind of mediator that the lawyers want. The mediator must have sufficient attributes and experience to have been made the choice of lawyers from different jurisdictions. For the mediator it is particularly vital to consider how he is going to be seen by the lawyers or parties coming from a culture he does not share.

Linguistic and Cultural items

Obviously parties that are dealing with cross-border disputes have got to select a language to use in the course of the mediation. It is a feature of western arrogance, or a particular blend of chauvinism and the lawyer's narcissism – or perhaps it is just the author - to think (or even pretend) that everyone speaks English or uses it in the same way. Some people speak English better than others. Some who say they speak English have varying ability to deal with a large vocabulary, or technical or legal expressions. Non-native speakers may be very confident in received English but have great difficulty with local or regional dialect, idiom, colloquialism, vernacular, and slang. Native English speakers need to have a high regard when addressing any audience for the percentage content of their speech which includes items falling into these categories.

Idiom in particular causes a lack of understanding in even good English speakers, and at the very least can be a distraction which leads to the hearer missing something that follows while he is trying to grasp the meaning of an unfamiliar phrase or reference which he has taken literally, as a starting point. This has been demonstrated over many years at international student mediation competitions conducted in English, where non-native speakers are clearly at a disadvantage unless this issue is either addressed or discounted.

Mediators need to think very carefully about whether they have any role in determining the choice of working language. Even if a mediator is a panel member of a mediation centre or institution, if he or she is in fact a foreign member, they may well not speak the local language.

The mediator must feel confident about the language in which the mediation is being conducted. If the mediator is not confident about that it may be a very good reason to have a co-mediator. A mediator may be selected for his or her subject matter expertise, experience or reputation, but none of these may extend to language skills, and the parties are happy to make the appointment on the basis they will attend with interpreters (which poses its own problems, of dependency, competency and specialisation).

Will the mediator, or where necessary the interpreter, be able to deal with regional accents and dialect; or local technical jargon? Will the way you put a question cause offence? If so, will the mediator be able to remove or explain it any by reframing in the desired cultural ambiguity?

The mediator working in a foreign language needs a number of qualities:

Understanding

He or she should be capable of breaking down issues to cross linguistic barriers, and needs to be aware of them or work confidently with an interpretive process –

- Common sense

The mediator should be responsible for the parties' understanding of the process and the content. It is a fundamental obligation which almost goes without saying. If it needs to be said, it needs to be put into the mediation agreement.

- Saving the face of parties and their lawyers

How do you ensure that people understand you without embarrassing them if they do not? In a 'face'-based jurisdiction or culture you have got to be immensely careful. You need to feel confident the mediator can take on this responsibility.

- Dealing with colloquialism

It may be that you are working in English and the standard of English of the opposing team is good, but the use of idiom, colloquialism, contemporary cultural referencing, jargon and slang would only be comprehensible to a native English speaker. Mediators can easily fall into the trap of becoming incomprehensible without even knowing by using phrases like: 'who is going to do the heavy lifting?' 'you need to dig deep.'

Unless the mediator is conscious of the problem he or she may do it without knowing they have already done so. Even if they are conscious, it is very easy for a native speaker of a language to make assumptions about the comprehension of the participants. This may be disadvantaging or embarrassing one side, or even both. If a party or their lawyer does not understand your meaning, they may think it too rude to embarrass you by raising the issue, and everyone then proceeds in ignorance.

The only way to avoid this is for the mediator to be conscious of the problem at the outset and to avoid using idiom – slang never – but also non-shared legal or technical jargon, or cultural referencing (derived from domestic media).

- Same expression – different meaning

There may be technical or legal expressions which are not shared across the jurisdictions or have a slightly different meaning. The lawyers opposite may still use generations-old legal Latin maxims which have now faded from use in the courts of England and Wales. We have to fall back on translation, which may vary and often does not accurately reflect the concept embodied by the original maxim.

Interpreters

The problem with interpreters – even simultaneous translation – is that you have no control over what the interpreter is saying. As a young barrister I learned a valuable lesson during a case in which I was junior counsel for the defence of a man at the Central Criminal Court. Old Bailey cases are serious. We had been going for three days when I felt a tug on my gown, and a member of the public told me that the interpreter, who was translating a dialect of Urdu, was not doing so properly as he lived in the same village. I had to bring the matter to the attention of the judge, the trial was abandoned and the jury discharged. I have been wary of interpreters ever since.

Test interpreters where you can – without being rude – take them to one side and ask about their experience of the process and how comfortable they are with the technical expressions used in mediation. Invest in some humour. A good way to test the competency of an interpreter is whether they understand a joke in the designated language. This enables you to see not only skill in translation but also cultural nuancing. The translation of a language – particularly, but not exclusively English – is more than just a reproduction of the words used, but involves colour, tone, depth, and the specific choice of words to be used in a language rich in vocabulary, or one that is stratified with layers of cultural appropriateness.

Is the mediator entitled to say to the lawyer or the party that the interpreter is not good enough? What impact will that have on the perception of the mediator? It may have to be done. Alternatively, the mediator may have to condition his or her own vocabulary to make the words used as simple as possible to shut out alternative meaning. The irony is that introducing an interpreter into the proceedings will have an impact on the way that you speak yourself.

The one area that is absolutely vital is to make sure that a non-English speaking party – even those who speak English but for whom it is not their first language – understands the nature of any settlement properly, that they understand any obligations that arise under the settlement, and to ensure the settlement is sufficiently nuanced. By that I mean that it is not drafted in such a way that leaves it open to interpretation. And that more than anything is where the mediator has got to ram home the fact that language must be readily understood on a mutual basis, because if it is not understood on a mutual basis, the settlement is likely to break down, if not immediately then certainly in the future. The true nature of agreement is that both parties understand it in precisely the same way.

Cultural and Socio-cultural issues

It follows from what I have said so far that the influence of cultural values is enormous. It potentially affects all stages of mediation and probably more than we know or are willing to accept. If you think about it, it could include the degree of participation; it could also speak to whether a party is going to be proactive or reticent. If a party does not feel comfortable on a cultural level he or she will be far more reserved about engaging and the mediator will be stuck with dealing with a lawyer, who might be as much of an obstacle to settlement as if he were appearing in a courtroom.

So the mediator has got to work hard at preparing to deal with the cultural differences that appear in the room. And there may be more than two. Some years ago, I was asked to mediate a development dispute concerning a property in Dubai. In the room were the Canadian property owner, his American lawyer, me as the UK mediator, a local developer with his local lawyer, and a senior member of the family that had been provided with the land by the Sheikh, at whose request the development had been 'suggested'. As it turned out the cultural differences between the US and Arab lawyers were less than those between the Canadian client and the US lawyer.

The mediator needs to understand who is in the room and how they are viewing/perceiving what is going on. Another example concerned Japanese and Arab clients. They come from very different cultures. One believes in more direct, the other more indirect communication. The mediator may struggle particularly if the parties are effectively from cultural polar extremes.

Bias

It is very difficult as a mediator not to be drawn to the familiar, to what makes him or her comfortable. The chances are, if the mediator is dealing cross-culturally with others in the room, this will happen, and it will happen at a sub-conscious level. The advocate may not necessarily mind that, because there is a coping mechanism: the advocate knows that if trustworthy, the mediator is working towards getting the best available settlement for his or her client. That must be the case if the deal is going to be suitable to both parties.

However, in terms of perception, the mediator needs to be sufficiently disciplined not to gravitate towards the familiar, and to allow that to influence his or her approach to the unfamiliar. As an outsider he or she may be exercising a judgment, but a mediator is not entitled to do so and needs to guard against it.

Much is said by the mediation industry about the independence of mediators. The reality is that mediators are conditioned by their own biases. First the bias of being a lawyer, which makes someone analytical and evaluative, even if they are working in an environment which constrains them to be facilitative. In that sense facilitative merely means that the lawyer mediator is effectively being gagged and cannot speak freely. But all mediators evaluate all of the time. They have to. They wouldn't be able to do their work otherwise. The only thing is they are not allowed to express it. They are not allowed to express the fruits of their faculty and training as a lawyer in order to influence the outcome. Yet the lawyer mediator is desperate to do so since if the dispute sits within the context of a legal case, the mediator will know who is likely to win, or who the judge is likely to favour. I learned in Singapore there are two types of mediation advocate. The first wants an evaluative mediator to tell the other side their case is flawed and they will lose. The second already knows his or her case is a loser and he needs the mediator to tell the other side it is better than it really is.

The mediator knows who needs a nudge or a push to bring them to their senses, but they operate figuratively with either one or occasionally two hands tied behind their back. That, however, is the nature of the work, and operating in a cross-cultural dispute simply exacerbates the frustration a non-evaluative lawyer mediator feels.

While everyone can be satisfied with a settlement of the dispute, it is vital that the parties both understand and are aligned with what they have agreed. Part of the challenge of ensuring that is in reality the position can be met with proper preparation – you have to be as prepared as you can in the circumstances.

It may be that the parties in cross-cultural mediation should be kept apart unless there is a distinct purpose to bring them together, for example venting or option generation. What is the mediator trying to achieve? Proper preparation means the advocate should know what each caucus is for. But what are the plenaries for?

There I stress the great importance in using the flexibility of the dynamic movement within the process – the mediator can have everyone together, or lawyers only, or experts only, or parties only meetings, and more than one simultaneously. If the advocate can help to plan this with the mediator it may enable understanding of what the mediator is doing and why. The mediator will have limited ambitions for each caucus/meeting. He or she wants to tick the box and then move on. It helps with momentum; and it stops parties in the 'inactive' room from getting bored or disengaged or suspicious of practical bias.

Practical Preparation for International Work

Mediation advocacy may be an oxymoron, but the term was coined in order to contextualise lawyers' understanding, sell the familiar to lawyers who then gravitated towards the process, understood what was really needed, and learned how best to use it. In cross-border work there is an added dynamic to managing your own client and your own case. How do we make a win-win outcome in mediation when until now we are simply employed in securing a win for our own client?

How is acting for a party in international or cross-border mediation different from acting for a party in domestic mediation?

First, as I have indicated above, is the responsibility of the advocate/representative/lawyer to select the mediator. Choosing the right mediator is the most important role of the lawyer. That may sound perverse because the mediator is not the decision-maker. On the face of it the mediator should make little difference as to whether the parties come to settlement or not. But in fact the mediator has so much influence over what is going on that it is vital you choose a mediator that will suit your client's ambition and your intention.

Second, the difference between the role of mediator and that of the party representative tends to be magnified in order to cross cultural divides. Where the mediator is perfectly content to bring parties to settlement on such terms as are acceptable to them, the mediator has no part to play in deciding whether the settlement is fair, or appropriate, or comprehensive, or deals with the case or leaves it entirely in abeyance. The mediator may be entirely disapproving of the settlement. He or she may think the settlement is so imbalanced that it is likely to break down, but if that is what the parties choose to do it is no part of the mediator's role to be judgmental about the contents. Why? Because he or she does not know what is driving the parties to that settlement, or what is their motivation. Nor is it within the scope of the mediator's knowledge what is the true extent of the parties' ambition. The chances are that a party will ultimately keep a secret from the mediator, and particularly one from a foreign jurisdiction, and therefore keep that secret from their own lawyer. It simply doesn't matter whether that is in fact the case, since so far as the mediator is concerned, as long as the parties get to yes his or her task is completed.

The role of the mediation advocate is different. Your task is to get the best available settlement for your client. Most of your money is earned in trying to discover what that is likely to be. Because most of the time it has nothing to do with the pleaded case. Most of the time the arena for settlement and the potential for option generation does not arise out of the case at all. It may arise out of existential threats to your ability to win the case, but for the most part the case is one small part only of the broader vista that your client can see, but at the outset you cannot.

Ordinarily I will say to a domestic audience of lawyers that because the mediator and the advocate have different objectives, there will come a point on the road which they share as part of the journey where their paths inevitably will diverge. At that point the mediator is no longer your friend, however much rapport the mediator has built, and however open you and your client and indeed the mediator have been because at that point you come under a duty to your client that the mediator does not share.

The irony is that in a cross-border mediation you need the mediator to be your friend more than ever. You need to work even more closely with the mediator than otherwise you would in your domestic environment, where you can always fall back on your knowledge of your jurisdiction, procedural rules, your client's true interests and, most important of all, your BATNA. The BATNA is the stick you will be leaning on in the context of what you are trying to achieve. If you have formulated it correctly that is your minimum target. If you secure that and then seek more, that is the mark of a sophisticated mediation advocate who is in possession of all the information he or she needs in order to secure the best available settlement.

With mediation advocacy operating at an international level the problems are the variables and uncertainties of what the mediator is doing, particularly if he or she comes from your opponent's or a third party culture.

If you are operating in another jurisdiction the least you need to know is that the mediator who has been selected is going to do the kind of job you need that person to do. Reverting to what was previously discussed about mediator selection, does the advocate want an interventionist, robust, commercially-oriented person, or a subject matter expert? Is it better to have someone who is laissez-faire and passive, allowing the advocate to get on with his or her own agenda? Sometimes that might be very attractive – to be able to send them off to seek an answer to a problem, or justification for a position so that I can understand. It is a nice idea as an advocate - you tasking the mediator, rather than the other way around.

Part of the mediator's role is to identify on a spectrum running from contentious to collaborative where the lawyer sits, and what it will take to bring the lawyer into collaborative mode. For example your opponent may be an aggressive American lawyer who still regards negotiation as a form of combat, who religiously uses Sun Tzu (*the Art of War*), and who thinks the outcome is a prize to be won by him for his client. He doesn't recognize mediation as a two-way process in which to succeed in getting the outcome the client needs, he must work out what the other side needs and find a way to help them have it.

How do you deal with that situation? It is alien to your culture, which is essentially built on being reasonable; it is alien to mediation, or at least your view of it. How do you convert an aggressive opponent into one that will work with you? You need to recruit the mediator to help with that sort of task. In preparing you can gain information about your opponent using the web to get background on him. That should give you your opposite number's professional qualifications, education, experience, work history, negotiating style or experience in the form of description or recommendation, reputation, areas of professional expertise; and that is quite a lot of information to have about someone even before you meet them. There is nothing sinister in this. In my view it should be a natural and distinct part of your preparation for at least the negotiation phase.

You will have chosen your mediator, whether robust and activist or passive and laissez-faire, according to those qualities you think are appropriate to your case and your client.

You will know about your opponent before you know about the mediator. It may be that you can choose a mediator, very specifically, who can act as a foil against the negotiating qualities of the lawyer on the other side. Here is an opportunity to think about engagement even at the outset of the mediation.

I am not necessarily concerned about mediator bias. I want to *exploit* the reality of mediator bias if I am to regard the mediator as a semi-detached member of my team. You can then approach the problem of mediator bias by simply saying it doesn't matter. Acknowledge that it exists then discount it. If that is a practical approach it doesn't matter whether the mediator has a subconscious educational or cultural or jurisdictional bias, gravitating towards the familiar, for example civil codes or common law, western or eastern facing: you are going to be choosing the mediator (and his or her likely biases) and therefore the bias doesn't matter. *You make it work for you.*

After this grounding in the type of jurisdictional questions which cross-border mediation gives rise to, when preparing for mediation, the advocate is no longer interested in the mediator. You are solely interested in the other side. You want to know about the other side's jurisdiction because by finding that out will tell you what their expectation is in terms of mediation process: in terms of the enforceability of the settlement; in terms of any regulatory requirements that feed into the settlement or by which the process is to be conducted. You need to investigate the impact of the other side's jurisdiction on their authority to settle. So you are focusing now on them, and not the process and not the mediator.

That will lead into the choice of language, and all of those same factors mentioned above in the mediator selection. In the choice of language where do the advantages and disadvantages lie? Obviously, you would prefer to choose your own language. Your own primary language is always the language in which you should mediate. However, since you have a duty to your client a more appropriate question is what the best language for your client is, or better still, what is the language which is most conducive to getting an acceptable settlement. We assume you and your client share the same primary language. If you don't there will have been a good reason for you being instructed.

You need to make sure you are not going to be under a disadvantage linguistically in acting in a cross-border mediation.

If no common language is agreed or the use of language in common is not at a high enough level you must consider the use and effectiveness of an interpreter.

Party management is probably too important to be left to the mediator. We sell mediation to clients on the basis that it is quicker and cheaper, a more flexible approach and a more desirable outcome. And one of the things we say to our clients is they retain control, that mediation provides party empowerment in a way in which no other process does, and they fully understand the process because it is theirs. Having sold mediation on that basis is, of course a lie, because either the mediator or the lawyers are controlling the process.

When operating on an international basis, there is an opportunity for the client to seek true empowerment, and it is perfectly open to you as the lawyer representing your client to bring this about by identifying what it is that you (your client) wants to happen during the course of the mediation. The mediation advocate has an excuse. He can say to the mediator, "Oh, we don't do things like that where we come from. Plenary session? Sorry, what's that? You want us to sit in the same room together? We don't do that. Caucus? You mean you're going to speak to the other side secretly in their room and we're not going to be there? We don't do that."

You can adapt the process to what your client truly wants by saying to the mediator this is our requirement. In this jurisdiction this is how we do things, and we fully expect this to happen, and simply because we are mediating somewhere else with you that doesn't mean we don't expect you to meet our expectations.

This is neither to denigrate the process nor exaggerate the possibilities available, but is to be provocative.

So look at the opportunities available in a cross-border situation that are not normally there in a domestic dispute. Because what I am really talking about is the value system that attaches to cross-cultural or cross-border mediation.

First there is the wonderful opportunity of using the mediation process to reduce or negate the suspicion of miscommunication. Disputes – particularly cross-cultural disputes – arise more often than not out of miscommunication and a misunderstanding of the values which someone is going to receive and analyse information which is being provided, perhaps for the first time in the dispute. This may extend to the way in which an assertion is put or what is being said about it. At its lowest level mediation is a terrific opportunity to provide clarification to all parties about the subject matter of the dispute, its history, context and impact down to that day. This is particularly important if the settlement is going to come from a reintegration of the parties' relationship. This requires counsel to manage the drama in conjunction with the mediator.

Second, the client is being offered a means of opening up possibilities which might be closed to people that transact business, or deal with a dispute that has arisen, either as a matter of distance or as a matter of misunderstanding. It gives the advocate option generation without selection bias caused by limited information. It has the advantage of calling together those who already have an apprehension that the way they see things is different. Even at its most basic level there is an easy explanation as to how people fall in terms of the psychology of people viewing things differently: it acknowledges and clarifies cognative dissonance.

In the same way described above, in discussing the cultural proclivity of one of the groups to rely upon the use of questions and answers in the exploration phase of the mediation in order to understand someone's value system, so you don't have to be a psychologist to understand that when you're dealing with somebody from another culture they are going to be predisposed to think differently from you. The mediator provides an acknowledgement of good faith differences and offers validation to both parties in order to deliver empathy as a vehicle for carrying people forward with a sense of common understanding about what is important and what it will take to solve the problem.

Time

It is worth considering the impact of time when working in a different time zone, or when participants are operating online contemporaneously from different zones.

If the advocate needs to acclimatise, then he or she must make sure the timetable allows time to deal with potential jet lag, travel delays, the client's and other attendees' travel arrangements, last-minute pre-mediation conferences and dealing with the mediator as host. The effects of jet-lag on a long haul journey may last up to three days.

The opposite number may wish to play local host to the advocate and the mediator, and this is likely to be the case in Japan or China. If so a day should be built in for this, as the mediation will not start without a getting-to-know-you protocol.

If you are working online contemporaneously with participants from different zones do have the courtesy to recognise how late it may be for those in the East, and how early for those in the West. The mediation may not always be Eurocentric, and it would be inappropriate without prior agreement to expect others to work well into the night where they are, or unsociably early in the morning. Agree regular breaks away from the screen, and otherwise have regard to the ideas in the chapter on mediation in the online world.[10]

Option Generation

Once you understand that you are working in a cross-cultural environment in which all of those factors under discussion come into play, for the party representative, even in terms of preparation, you need to consider from where the solution is most likely to come. Who will be the 'paying' party, and will they make the first offer? Are you confident about participating in option generation, on the basis that the eventual outcome will be derived either from the case itself, or the development of a transaction based on a bargain for the payment in whole or in part for goods, services or in recompense for an action or omission. If the solution is not going to come from such a transaction, will it flow from a transfer of property or from the reintegration of a trading or some other kind of ongoing relationship? In terms of option generation, that probably covers most options merely among these choices.

If the settlement agreement is going to derive from the case itself in circumstances where there is no ongoing trade or transactional relationship, preparation must include focusing on enforcement of the agreement as if it were a judgment. The relevant legal requirements in both jurisdictions must be understood - the advocate's own and the other party's. Also it is likely to some extent that the cultural nuances in the professional or legal culture of the person on the other side will have an effect.

Preparing for an effective settlement the advocate's thoughts should revert to enforceability within the client's chosen jurisdiction, which will be a matter of local law and procedure. He or she will have made themselves aware well in advance of the mediation whether that jurisdiction is a signatory to the Singapore Convention, and if so whether and when it ratified, and whether or not the Convention has yet been brought into effect there. In that regard, the advocate must check whether the agreement your client may enter is caught by any of the carve out provisions in Articles 5 or 8.

---

10 See p41.

If it is simply a matter of money or money's worth, be careful to have regard to the psychological impact of large sums in a small-value currency. It will affect the advocate as well as the client without familiarity with the use of the currency being used in the mediation. Be generally aware of relevant exchange rates, particularly if working in commonly internationalised currencies – US dollars, euros, Swiss francs. Protect the client from offers coming in soft currencies, or those that are particularly volatile, or carrying high inflation. Given a choice of currency, look for stability and pairing with internationally recognised benchmark currencies.

If there is to be new transactional business, for example a new contract which replaces that in dispute, then again the legal requirements must be examined. It may be as simple and generic as checking local legal requirements to identify and ensure compliance with the four key factors that you're going to need to know about the other person's jurisdiction:

- is this transaction going to be lawful?
- is it going to be sufficiently certain for the Court to give effect to the intentions of the parties at the time they entered into it should it be called upon to do so?
- is it going to be workable as a matter of practicability?
- is it going to be enforceable on its face?

These are the minimum issues the advocate needs to know about the transactional law in the jurisdiction or the hinterland of the lawyer on the other side. Because these same things will occupy the mind of that lawyer.

If the options for settlement to be generated arise out of a property transfer then rather obviously the jurisdictional regulation or law that applies to the transfer of property in the other jurisdiction is relevant. The advocate needs to know that for enforcement; for registration, and more importantly whether a settlement is possible which is going to involve the transfer of property with the information available at the beginning of the mediation? Even working domestically in the instance that the solution to the problem that the mediation has brought the parties to is a property transfer, then a search against the title will be needed, with a check for encumbrances on the title, the interests of other stakeholders, particularly mortgagees, and the hierarchy or ranking of other creditors than the client.

In transactional work it may be necessary to know about the corporate structure of the other party in much more detail than you already have. This will extend to governance, compliance and an understanding of any local regulatory regime. Practitioners will already have in mind anti-money laundering and anti-corruption legislation, both local and international, should their client be participating, whether or not by design, in unlawful activity.

If the options that are being generated flow from a reintegration of the parties' relationship, it is necessary to know how that is going to work, possibly in much wider terms than is possible to prepare for. But this is the point at which to reissue the warning that in the other jurisdiction it may be necessary to know about the hierarchies on the other side: more than just corporate structure. Try and uncover beneficial interests, family or wider social ordering and tribal authority.

Because that goes to the heart of the matter. How you understand the true nature and interests of the opposite party? This refers to beneficial interests because it is something that covers the hinterland of stakeholders, or family, or tribal, or state, or governmental interests that may not be apparent simply by looking at what is there on paper.

How does the advocate investigate these things? One thing that is possible is to make use of the fact that the mediation advocate on the other side is most likely a lawyer and you are a lawyer, and you have a common fraternity. Or else if the case is going to turn on the testimony of experts, the fraternity of experts may be used: if the true question between the parties is a technical question and the outcome sits within the case and nowhere else. In that instance the advocate will want an expert in the mediation and he wants to make use of the experts on the other side. If I mediate I take the experts from both sides and I put them in the room and I say up to today you have been paid to deliver your opinion to support your client, but today and today only you are being paid to see if you can come together, limit the issues between you, and find a workable solution which is subject matter related.

That's when I'm the mediator. But as an advocate I put my expert on show in the plenary session, since my expert is there to explain where the other side's case is fundamentally flawed, and his or her job is to undermine the confidence of the other side before the negotiation starts.

Sometimes you find the experts are actually driving the differences between the parties, particularly if there is a variation in professional standards and practice across the jurisdictions. There may equally be deference or resistance to deference to a Western expert, which may be an expression of political, cultural or historical referencing.

Dealing with foreign counsel

Engaging with counsel in international work the advocate may be faced with someone who seems ridiculously aggressive and completely out of keeping with his or her own view of professional behaviour.

A difficulty to face is that it can be unclear whether the problem is one of cultural referencing or whether it is simply the individual. If the latter, the advocate can use the mediator to defend his or her position from unwarranted and aggressive behaviour. The mediator ought to ask of that issue, "do you think this is going to make it easier to get a settlement or less because what happens if your behaviour drives them away," and a competent mediator immediately goes into BATNA testing mode in the other room, while in this room the client will think the mediator is actively protecting his or her interests.

The corollary is that the mediation advocate's role is not really to be a belligerent advocate or even a combative negotiator because the mediator blunts the negotiation anyway by modifying directness. The mediator either accepts what is said or not and goes to the other side and reframes and puts it in the best light – or maybe doesn't put it at all: what the mediator is saying in the other room is not known. The advocate must just trust the mediator unless or until there is a divergence of interest.

Even then, it doesn't mean it is right to trust the mediator less. It means that the advocate has his or her own client interests to protect. In an international context this is apparent really because of the cultural barriers to negotiation. Do they matter? I think they do. But even if they matter a great deal, you can use the mediator as a cushion, that is to soften the landing of a disharmonious attitude. After all, the chances of speaking directly across the table during the negotiation phase are not very high unless the mediation has reached deadlock and the mediator has chosen to bring the parties together in order to try to break it.

This does raise a question: since for most of the negotiation phase the mediator uses shuttle diplomacy and passes from private room to private room, why does it matter whether the advocate has an awareness of the cultural concerns which may have an impact on the outcome? It is possible that if negotiating with a foreign lawyer, cultural differences may be seen as an obstacle to communication, since there may be unfamiliar laws, or unfamiliar ideologies which can be equally as important, or governmental policy or religiosity. At the very least these may be a complication. If they are there, the advocate cannot just pretend they are not, so how to deal with them?

Awareness of perhaps four very specific things is needed:

First whether the cultural differences are going to have an impact on communication. That may be as simple as language, as previously discussed; it may be more nuanced than that but the advocate must be aware and ensure that through the mediator there is a channel for communication that works.

Second, it is necessary to have an understanding of what is acceptable or not acceptable in the behaviour of the advocate and his or her client when in the presence of the other side, because what are judged to be behaviours which are unusual or unacceptable or even incomprehensible but, which to the other side are completely normal, are likely to have a mirror held up against them. Value judgments are important and may have wider implications, not the least of which is understanding.

So, for example, in the world of nepotism, if you work in the Gulf you will realise pretty quickly that the family is everything. The Arabs even have a word for the way they use nepotism. It's called 'wasta'. The best translation from Arabic is 'influence'. Wasta is probably going to mean that a family member is related to a member of the Ruling Family, or maybe a member of your family is related by marriage through somebody else to somebody else, and that is how you get the job. Nepotism is perfectly acceptable in the

Arab world because Arab employers will say 'if we have a structure which is based on bringing in family members, we know first of all that you can trust them and secondly, that they will be loyal.' This is cultural behaviour, which is entirely acceptable for them, but from a western perspective the use of nepotism, the use of influence is simply bordering on the corrupt or at least it is certainly not leading by meritocracy or by competence or talent or qualification or experience. The latter requires on the job training and further education. The idea of starting on the shop floor and working your way up to management is completely unheard of in the GCC.

If a young person comes back from a foreign university as a graduate or postgraduate then they will ordinarily be parachuted into a senior position in the management of a company irrespective of whether their academic qualifications have anything to do with the particular job. That's the natural way in which they operate and it is perfectly acceptable behaviour, which at the same time would be difficult to understand from many western perspectives, particularly in regulated organisations or governmental entities or agencies.

The third thing is that cultural considerations may influence both the form and the substance of the eventual deal, so if the deal is going to be transaction based, cultural considerations may well have to be taken into consideration in the way the outcome is formulated. What may look like anti-competitive arrangements in certain jurisdictions may be perfectly acceptable where the negotiation takes place.

Finally, culture can influence the way people act whilst they are at the bargaining table. This is not about the honour culturalist banging the table and screaming and shouting. What matters is their view of what is important. I expect a mediator to come into my room at some point fairly early on in the process, and say what is important to you? It is a question I always ask, because the answer is extremely useful of itself where hopefully, you're beginning to discover what the client really wants, and as a mediator I would say "okay, is there anything else" or "is there something else that can be exchanged for that I can try and trade?"

In a cross-cultural context, the mediator may be surprised by party priorities or by the general approach as to what is really important, because in one room they may be looking at a case-based outcome, and in the other room they may be looking at a relationship-based outcome. Therefore, it is as well that in preparation advocates need to know whether cultural referencing is going to push opposing parties in any particular direction or not, simply so that the option generation process is assisted.

Using apology in cross-cultural work

The importance of the cultural and linguistic approach to the use of apology is such that it should be regarded as a self-contained subject. We often use apologies in mediation as a vehicle where something which is of no value or no cost (or low cost) to the giver, may be received as something of great value by the recipient. Of course, I advance that as very much a cultural assumption.

Be aware that apologies mean different things in different cultures, and that these can be used in different ways. Apologies should always be used and worded with great care because conceptually they are of great value.

I used to think the variation of importance in which the apology was regarded was entirely semantic, after all we recognise an apology as an unqualified expression of regret – almost sorrow – for what has happened passing from the giver to the recipient. The apology explicitly recognises harm which the recipient has suffered or loss sustained. It may fall short of acknowledging blame or liability. So, you have one side going into an open session and saying, "We are very sorry it has come to this". Is that an apology? It may be an expression of regret but there is no recognition of the position of the recipient or addressee. Or they may say, "We are very sorry that you are so upset. Apology? No. An apology in western culture is the offering of regrets for behaviour, which is now implicitly either admitted, or some degree of fault is conceded. Invariably an apology is attributed to an individual rather than an institution although sometimes of course it can be used by an institution, for example in defamation or in libel claims. That may extend to corporate liability in personal injury or clinical negligence cases.

But not all cultures see apologies in the same way.

In particular there is a distinction between an individualistic culture like the United States or the United Kingdom and the collectivist culture like Japan or China who view apologies in a very different way. Dealing with lawyers and parties on the other side who come from a completely different culture, the advocate must be extremely careful of the words he or she chooses to use, not just what the intention is, but also what he or she is trying to project to them. It depends how they receive it. As in most things in the negotiating phase, including providing information, the meaning of a message how is received and not how it is given.

Famously in the Citygroup case in Japan, recounted by Michael Leathes[11] – a US executive had to respond to substantial regulatory breaches. The Chief Executive Officer, Charles Prince, went on television; he bowed before the television cameras and apologised deeply for his or her company's mistakes. So far as members of the Japanese audience was concerned, they didn't see this as an emotional exercise in the acknowledgement of personal liability but they saw it as the minimum requirement necessary for the reintegration of the relationship of the bank with Japan.

If formulating and using an apology, particularly where it is perceived as a matter of real value within the bargaining framework, it is necessary to understand how it will be received, what the intention should be, and how powerful it can be in setting the mood of the whole mediation. Even if it does not form part of the trade, sending a message at the start of the mediation which ameliorates the whole situation may create a tone which goes to the heart of whether a deal is possible, and whether it will be possible to draw a

11 Michael Leathes *Negotiation – Things Corporate Counsel Need to Know but Were Not Taught* Wolters Kluwer 2017

line under what has happened in the past. To that end these considerations may be important:

Consider the recipient or recipients. Design words so they have the maximum intended effect.

Consider whether the apology is singular, therefore passing from the client to the recipient, or mutual, where might words denoting regret in return be reasonably expected?

When is the optimum time to raise the need for apology?

- In pre-mediation discussion with the mediator
- In the written position or interest statement
- In the opening plenary session as a means of setting the tone
- In the opening plenary session as an agenda item
- In a private caucus with the mediator in discussing option generation
- Within the negotiation phase

Note that each will have a different impact and may well affect the momentum of the process differently.

Do not demand an apology from the other party if you know it will be very difficult for them to give it. This may be because of cultural resistance, for example from Chinese. Or it may be that a defendant's insurer is worried this will be a precursor to an admission of liability which they are not prepared to concede. Try to formulate an expression which is agreeable, and which will be acceptable to the client, if necessary explaining the other party's difficulty.

If there is real value in the client securing an apology, consider with care what that value may be in the context of an overall settlement, and specifically to what use the client may put it if it is reduced to writing as a formal statement that expresses regret or remorse for a mistake, offence, or wrongdoing. Unlike saying sorry, an apology is a more formal and structured way of acknowledging responsibility for one's actions. It involves admitting fault and taking full responsibility for the mistake or offense. In without prejudice negotiations, such a statement can be a powerful tool in bringing catharsis to the client and allowing him or her to draw a line and move on with their life.

Chapter 7
Ethical Dilemmas and Cross-Cultural Sensibilities

It is fairly common for advocates to face ethical problems in mediation, including conundrums in intercultural or cross-border work caused either by unfamiliarity or stereotyping. The difficulties faced by lawyers, in particular, are generally different to those of the mediator, although they sometimes overlap. The subject matter is broad, and of importance both to professional and non-professional party representatives. The latter may struggle to look for answers to ethical problems and may even fail to recognise the nature of the problem. That difficulty generally stems from the danger of thinking that there are no rules in mediation, which is certainly not the case.

When we stray away from the safety of the civil litigation framework and find ourselves in territory which is not necessarily familiar to us, it is quite common that something may occur either between you and your client, or between you and the mediator, or something is said in the presence of the mediator which causes in you a metaphorical alarm bell to start ringing (or ought to do so).

Ethical problems cause you to panic, particularly in circumstances where you feel that you are on your own. This is equally true of mediators since the practice of mediation as a neutral can be a very solitary profession, but I wish to focus on what the advocate should consider and where support is available.

Because you may not know what to do, the first thing to remember is there are plainly both procedural and substantive rules that govern mediation. We are not operating in a vacuum. We need to be aware of where to find such rules and see what assistance they provide. Mediation tends to throw up surprises, both for the mediator and party representative, as the path we tread veers away – sometimes quite sharply – from the intended direction of travel formed in pre-mediation planning. Very likely this will throw you off balance, particularly in circumstances where you had felt in your own mind that you had some sort of a strategy for the day leading to a satisfactorily negotiated outcome, and one that was controlled by you. Something, therefore, has come along which has undermined that planning, and creates an ethical dilemma.

Start by looking at the first place where we encounter a set of rules which are designed to cover the particular process: the mediation agreement, which is plainly both in fact and law a contract between the parties intended to govern the procedural aspects of the day. This sets out the rights and obligations of the parties, for example to attend in good faith with authority to settle, issues of confidentiality, and the powers of and protection for the mediator. It is a tripartite contract because it is not between just the parties, but the mediator as well, and invariably in addition the mediation service provider separately if there is one. Beyond that, everyone who participates in the mediation, even only as an observer, should sign a schedule to the mediation agreement to confirm they will be bound by the confidentiality which covers the process like an umbrella, the entire process being either confidential or privileged or the subject of without prejudice negotiation depending on the jurisdiction in which you are working: there will either be a legal privilege which is vested in the parties, and also separately in the mediator for the purpose of protecting the process, and without which the parties would not trust it, or a legally binding contractual duty of confidentiality actionable as a breach of confidence.

Where the jurisdiction permits, the usual without prejudice rules apply as if it was any other kind of negotiation within litigation or as a precursor to a claim, to the extent they are embodied in local law which, presumably, governs the mediation unless a cross-border agreement saying otherwise is in place.

The mediation agreement, probably put into a standard form either by the mediation service provider or by the mediator himself or herself, will set out in as much detail as is felt necessary the powers of the mediator and the obligations of the parties, either general or specific. These may concern the control of behavioural issues specific to the conduct of the parties. Such minimum guidelines are there to protect the integrity of the process and defend the position of the mediator and his service provider, since the mediation may be construed as a quasi-judicial proceeding but one that is effectively outside the remit of immediate supervision by the Court unless things go badly wrong.

If the mediation is at the Court's direction and there has been a court referral, then irrespective of the confidentiality provisions attaching to the agreement, the Court does exercise supervisory jurisdiction at the very least in respect of the behaviour of lawyers who are either its officers or otherwise owe a duty to the court in which they practice. Here their ethical obligations are no greater and no less than their general ethical standards regulated by the Court and by their professional bodies: what you would not do as a lawyer, you would not do as a lawyer in mediation[1]. The fact that you feel

1 The Bar 'Code of Conduct' for England and Wales sets out ten core duties for Barristers. CD2, CD3, CD4, CD5, CD6, CD7, CD8 and CD10 are probably all potentially engaged in acting as advocates within a mediation.

CD1 You must observe your duty to the court in the administration of justice [CD1].

CD2 You must act in the best interests of each client [CD2].

CD3 You must act with honesty, and with integrity [CD3].

CD4 You must maintain your independence [CD4].

CD5 You must not behave in a way which is likely to diminish the trust and confidence which the public places in you or in the profession [CD5].

CD6 You must keep the affairs of each client confidential [CD6].

the process is more informal than a court or a tribunal hearing – either by design or by the approach of a particular mediator - does not entitle you to relax your standards of conduct and behaviour, and this would include the improper use of mediation as a vehicle for delay, or seeking inappropriately the discovery of business information or private matters having commercial value in the absence of a genuine willingness to settle. You have a continuing duty to advise independently, honestly and with integrity, promoting equality and upholding the rule of law.

An obvious example concerns what happens during the course of the negotiation phase: are you, in the course of negotiating, able to say something either to the mediator or to the other side which is not strictly true? This normally involves the limit of your authority on the kind or extent of the offer that you are prepared to make in the course of bargaining. So very typically, when you are negotiating there may come a point where you say to the mediator, "We are prepared to go this far and no further," yet you know perfectly well - because you have instructions to that effect - that there is or may actually be more to concede or exchange by way of bargain.

CD7 You must provide a competent standard of work and service to each client [CD7]

CD8 You must not discriminate unlawfully against any person [CD8].

CD9 You must be open and co-operative with your regulators [CD9].

CD10 You must take reasonable steps to manage your practice, or carry out your role within your practice, competently and in such a way as to achieve compliance with your legal and regulatory obligations [CD10].

The Law Society delegated its regulatory powers to the Solicitors Regulation Authority in 2007. Solicitors currently provide legal service under the Solicitors Regulation Authority Code of Conduct 21st version (2019 October) which contains six mandatory principles, ('SRA Principles'), supplemented by mandatory outcomes ('SRA outcomes') and 'indicative behaviours' ('SRA indicative behaviours') that all solicitors should comply with:

SRAP 1: To uphold the constitutional principle of the rule of law, and the proper administration of justice;

SRAP 2: To uphold public trust and confidence in the solicitors' profession and in legal services; provided by authorised persons;

SRAP 3: To act with independence;

SRAP 4: To act with honesty;

SRAP 5: to act with integrity;

SRAP6: to act in a way that encourages equality, diversity and inclusion.

While at present mediation is not the provision of a legal service, acting as an advocate in mediation falls within the normal course of a solicitor's professional practice and it is unlikely the general SRAP requirements can be disapplied.

When you consider the context of negotiation, nobody would say that you were in breach of an ethical duty simply because you were trying to bargain for a better deal without showing the whole of your hand. But you must be cautious in departing from a truthful position. For that very reason it is unwise to tell the mediator what your 'bottom line' is and it is even more unwise for the mediator to ask of you that question, principally because the answer is actually more fluid than perhaps you would imagine, or have been instructed, particularly if the negotiation moves much more quickly than you thought would be the case beforehand, and you find yourself standing on a trap door over your authority which falls away in the dark below should the trap be sprung and the door opened. By the same token a mediator should resist the temptation to ask either you or your client a question in open session which may give rise to the need to answer differently depending whether or not the opposite party is present.

It is therefore a matter of common sense - or should I say professional good sense - what you should and should not be doing as a representative of a party where you have a dilemma about what you may say to the mediator, either on that party's behalf or about him.

For many years my own Code of Conduct of the Bar of England and Wales stated expressly that a barrister must not lie to a mediator and that this was a separate and distinct disciplinary offence. That has now been removed – of course not on the basis it is now permissible to lie to the mediator - but that the situation is covered by the general conduct rules attaching to the way in which a member of the Bar should behave. It is covered by the broad sanctions attaching to 'conduct unbecoming of a barrister',[2] and it matters not what your home profession is, but if by your conduct you bring your profession into disrepute that is a matter of professional discipline and it is something of which you must be conscious irrespective of the fact you are now in mediation rather than litigation. Professionals are usually left to their own good judgment, and if they require help will know where it may be found.

The danger for the professional advocate is that ethical problems may develop because you are working much more closely with the client in mediation than in litigation, since in having concern for his business affairs and his social arrangements, and the kind of relationship that is ongoing between him and the other side, and whether that is going to be perfected or extended or operate in the future at all, your client may well tell you things as his counsel that he would not need to tell you in the course strictly of commercial litigation; and more particularly, you may find yourself asking your client to give you information which you certainly would not want to ask about in the course of litigation.

Once you have received that information, on occasion, the client may instruct you in a way that leads to your being professionally embarrassed in the face of your ethical responsibility not to deceive. You should advise your client that if the settlement agreement takes effect in law as a contract, it can be impeached and set aside like any other contract, for misrepresentation,

2 See the specific items at note 1.

mistake, undue influence or duress at the instance of the innocent party, irrespective of the fact it came about through mediation. Neither the party representative, nor the mediator can become a conduit for fraud.

Mediators are not only bound by the mediation agreement but may also be regulated by the mediation service provider, which will likely either have its own code of conduct or adopt the European Code of Conduct for Mediators which applies to mediators and by extension, should apply to mediation advocates where relevant. The mediation process and all actors associated with it are also caught by anti-money laundering regulations,[3] and anti-bribery[4] and corruption legislation.[5] If you are acting in cross-border work, that will extend to legislation in foreign jurisdictions that may touch and concern your mediation, for example, the domestic anti-corruption legislation of the U.S.A., India and the Philippines.

In terms of your clients, there are provisions in respect of the legal duties, responsibilities and obligations of a company director[6] to keep records, ensure the payment of Corporation Tax and VAT and sign off company accounts and confirmation statements. You have to be confident that the company is not acting *ultra vires* in respect of its negotiations and authority, and that a single officer or director had the power to instruct you in the way that he or she did.

If the mediator recognises that there is a problem which is made manifest by the subject matter of the discussions he or she should step in and bring proceedings to a halt. There will be a clause in the mediation agreement empowering the mediator to do so without explanation. Yet this power is only exercised rarely when parties are represented, because the mediator may feel insulated from the perception of wrongdoing by your presence and that of advocates for the other participants.

One of the skills of the mediator is to suspend disbelief in the face of the obvious, this in order to create rapport with both sides, offer empathy to each and project neutrality. The bi-partial role of the mediator is designed to prevent obvious wrongdoing, such as allegations of fraudulent conduct, from undermining the process from the outset. However ethical issues which go directly to the continuing viability of the mediation need to be addressed. There is in such circumstances a line which, if crossed, will force the mediator to end the mediation. He or she cannot simply rely on the presence of party representatives to avoid the consequences of ethical issues.

---

3 S.328 Proceeds of Crime Act 2002; Serious Organised Crime and Police Act 2005; the third Money Laundering Directive (3MLD) of 15 December 2007, 2005/60/EC and extending to the 5th Directive (5MLD); The Money Laundering Regulations 2007 (SI 2007/2157); The Money Laundering (Amendment) Regulations 2012 (SI 2012/2298) and 2015 (SI 2015/11); The Money Laundering and Terrorist Financing and Transfer of Funds (Information on the Payer) Regulations 2017 (SI 2017/692) and (Amendment) Regulations 2019; The Proceeds of Crime (Money Laundering) (Threshold Amount) Order 2022.

4 The Bribery Act 2010

5 The Economic Crime and Corporate Transparency Act 2023

6 ss. 170-177 Companies Act 2006

As a mediator I have been confronted on occasion by party representatives – both solicitor and counsel – who were willing to assure me that my concerns about what I believed was going on were misplaced, exaggerated or imagined, and that I was both insulated and protected by their own presence. Professional advocates should not allow the mediator to be put in such a position, and subject only to the limit of their instructions, I would encourage them to have frank, though confidential, discussions with the mediator. A party can be motivated into agreeing this by not wishing to be seen as the one causing the mediator such problems, and will want to be seen as working in cooperation with the mediator in order to get the best deal: after all, there is something in the old joke about selecting a mediator, where you don't care how neutral the mediator is as long as he's on your side! If that is true, even on an elementary level, if you want the mediator to be on your side for whatever reason, and whatever you think that's worth, you are not going to behave, or permit your client to behave, in such a way that undermines what the mediator is doing, alienates and pushes him or her more towards being empathic with the other side. In that sense the process regulates itself, as long as the mediator is strong enough to intervene to stop bad behaviour if it happens.

Ultimately the provision in a standard form mediation agreement which empowers the mediator to bring the process to an end without explanation operates as an ethical safety valve, and on the very rare occasions it might be used the mediator will feel that the process has been compromised because something unlawful is going on or because the behaviour of the advocates is such that they are in breach of their own professional code of conduct.

If the mediation had been mandated by the Court it is conceivable that a report back may be required in respect of the result. In stopping the process, unless the mediator is compelled by law to disclose the matter of concern, the duty of confidentiality under the mediation agreement remains in place, takes precedence, and the mediator should report only that the mediation failed to produce a settlement.

Even were there a settlement, I do not think that a court needs to know what the settlement is. It is no business of the Court to scrutinise or evaluate the settlement in a confidential process, and to the extent that England and Wales law requires the parties to file a Tomlin order to stay further proceedings, I take the view that any schedule detailing the terms of settlement arrived at in mediation should not be produced to the judge, and if asked for it you should politely resist the request.

If, as an advocate, you fall short of the required conduct and, in particular, if you fall short of either knowledge of your role and what your responsibilities are and as a consequence what your ethical behaviour needs to be, that seems likely to me to be grounds which may give rise to a claim of professional negligence. It is well worth making sure that you have access to the practice standards to which I have referred, and the telephone number of a senior practitioner who can give pragmatic mentoring advice. Ethical dilemmas in mediation are fairly common and that being the case you will need to have some idea of what you're going to do when (not 'if') you're faced with such a quandary. Consider where any potential danger lies at the outset of your instructions, and do not wait until you are caught in a real difficulty by surprise. Do not be complacent. Understand the professional and personal implications for you, and do not be shy of having a frank conversation with your client about what you may and may not do in the course of your mediation retainer.

International and cross-border work

For those engaged in representing parties in cross-border disputes or international mediation while there are common international ethical standards for mediators, shared standards for practitioners are still grounded in either domestic professional requirements or voluntary submission to the rules of international associations. For mediators practising internationally the ethical standards established by the European Code of Conduct for Mediators, the International Chamber of Commerce, the American Arbitration Association, the Chartered Institute of Arbitrators, Mediators Beyond Borders and the Asia Pacific Centre for Arbitration and Mediation, by way of example, together have a reasonably global reach. Mediation advocates who subscribe as members will operate under the prescribed standards and competencies developed by the Standing Conference of Mediation Advocates[7] and the International Mediation Institute.[8]

One of the significant problems you may face as an international practitioner in the context of common ethical issues is cross-cultural stereotyping. The great risk in mistaken stereotyping, either by you or by the mediator in your presence is that you wrongly attribute to people of another culture certain ideas and values that are not the case. Not only does this distort your analysis of the situation, but it may well give offence and even be seen as egregious by the opposing advocate. This is something one has to be particularly careful about in dealing with cross-border work, particularly if you are not operating in a common language; but even if you are operating in a common language, a non-native speaker may not recognise idiomatic expression, colloquialism or vernacular speech. You have an obligation – as much pragmatic as anything else - to make sure that both the mediator and the other side have a clear understanding of what it is that you and your clients are saying.

When retained (both as mediator and) as advocate in cross-border or cross-cultural work I am conscious of the need to edit out of my language vernacular expressions and idiom which might not be understood properly from the context by a non-native English speaker, and I hope that advocates on the other side of a case are doing exactly the same. Otherwise, I may be speaking to somebody who receives my communication on a literal basis when I don't intend that to be the case. This will also create a problem for the mediator because he or she may very well be trying to pass a message that I have conveyed in a way that I do not intend. Worse, he may be selling a settlement where the other side do not have the same understanding of what is and what is not being offered, particularly if there are contingencies attached to a proposal. I have to know that a mediator operating in a second

7 https://scmastandards.com/mediation-advocacy-standards/

8 https://imimediation.org/orgs/cag-maqaps/

language, or as a non-native English speaker, has a clear understanding of what my client is saying.

There may be a difference between a professional ethical obligation in this regard and the practical consequence of a mistake being made, but the consequences are not worth the risk. In my view there is a strong ethical obligation to make sure that if the parties get to an agreement there is a true consensus *ad idem* - a true meeting of minds - because otherwise the settlement is going to fall apart and it will do so very quickly because the lawyer or other party will go back and speak to somebody who wasn't present in the mediation and their reaction will be 'surely they didn't mean that ... surely you haven't signed up to that, because what you have signed up to is ridiculous!'

The one thing you want for your client is a durable settlement, thereby ending his or her problem on a basis acceptable to them. If the settlement is vitiated for mistake, or worse, misrepresentation arising out of a failure to understand the intended terms, the client's problem will rear its head again and either revert to the original dispute or alternatively, the Court will have to be asked to enforce the settlement under difficult and probably contested circumstances. You therefore need to be particularly concerned about making sure there is a clear understanding in cross-cultural or cross-border work, particularly when dealing with 'face-based' cultures.[9]

The other significant area which could give rise to ethical dilemmas as common as miscommunication of language concerns the possibility of giving offence to people on the other side. Imagine that you have said something in the course of the mediation when acting for your client and it has caused great offence across the table or in the other room and you do not know. You are going to be faced with either the party on the other side walking away or perhaps sometime later, subject to the provisions of confidentiality you might find yourself reported to your professional body for something of which you are completely unaware.

In either case you may find yourself prevented from even seeking advice about it by the confidentiality restrictions contained in the mediation agreement, and a client who might not waive confidence - or, where appropriate, privilege - because he thinks your action has undermined the mediation and damaged his position. You will need to understand the position under your professional retainer, any obligation owed to a participant under your code of conduct and your position vis a vis the mediator.

In considering with whom you may discuss your own professional dilemma the restrictions are real and not imagined. If you are working in a jurisdiction that attaches substantive privilege to the mediation process you are likely to have a considerable problem.[10] If there is privilege attaching to the mediation

9 See further in Chapter 6 on International work.

10 For example in the United States several jurisdictions have adopted the Uniform Mediation Act (the UMA), including Georgia, Hawaii, Idaho, Illinois, Iowa, Nebraska, New Jersey, Ohio, South Dakota, Utah, Vermont, Washington and Washington, D.C. One of the UMA's core directives is to ensure the ability for mediating parties to depend on the confidentiality of the proceedings and

and vested in the client it is quite likely that such a 'mediation privilege' will vest also in the mediator for the protection of the process. It is very unlikely that the mediator will waive privilege because it is vested in him to defend the process not to assist you, and therefore you have to understand the legal obligations that you are under in respect of confidentiality in your jurisdiction.

Reinforcements

Having worked out whether, and if so with whom you may share your dilemma, the best way to seek help is to call for reinforcements to consider the problem. I don't mean call for the cavalry, but I mean see if there are more senior people in your office or practitioners with whom you have a professional fraternity that you can ring up and speak to about your problem on a no names basis. Even if they have no immediate answer, by discussing the problem with a fellow professional it may become apparent what the appropriate course of action should be. Your local Bar or Law Society, or a like professional body may have an ethics helpline.

You should be able to talk to the mediator privately and in purely confidential terms which do not reflect badly in respect of your client's case. That can be very difficult sometimes, because it may be that your client has said something to you which you consider undermines your professional position. The fact that all mediation sits within the umbrella of confidentiality and apparently outside the immediate scrutiny of the Court does not change your professional position or obligation. You cannot lie to the mediator on the basis that your client has expressly instructed you to say something which you know to be false. You need to inform your client you cannot advance that, and if he insists you do so, you can no longer represent him. I think most of us, regardless of the jurisdiction in which we are working, would recognise that position as quite straightforward: if you are professionally embarrassed to the extent that you continue to act as a lawyer and as an advocate then you must withdraw. You don't need to tell the mediator why you're withdrawing but you do need to tell the mediator you can no longer go on. Most mediators will understand that there is a professional difficulty and if the client is willing to continue in the absence of his representative the mediation may proceed. There may need to be an adjournment for the client to seek new representation but at least the client will understand not to make the same mistake again. A mediator will have empathy with a party representative as somebody who has come under real professional difficulties, since he or she will be likely to understand the factual context; that being the case the mediator is perhaps also the obvious place where you should turn. Broadly speaking it should be a matter of associated professional common sense whether you are or you are not in difficulties, and unless you have been behaving badly yourself, mediators are drawn from the professions and will wish to be as supportive as they can.

---

accompanying communications. Indeed, the UMA protects all "mediation communications" from disclosure, and defines such communications broadly as any statement during the mediation or "made for purposes of" considering, conducting, or participating in a mediation. Uniform Mediation Act Sections 2, 4, U.L.A. MED §§ 2, 4 (2003).

Despite having practised in mediation for over 30 years, occasional surprises occur, and, subject to your obligation of confidentiality, you may think it best to have available the telephone numbers of two or three senior professional colleagues. I certainly do.

Ethical dilemmas

Here are some example problems – drawn from real situations[11] - that you may wish to consider. The answers will, I hope, emerge from our previous discussion.

> 1. You look at your alerter app law reports on your laptop on the way to mediation and realise that the Court of Appeal has just decided one of the crucial points in the client's case against you. What should you do about it? Does your answer make a difference if the other side is unrepresented, or represented by a non-lawyer?
>
> 2. Your solicitor says in booming voice loud enough for other side to hear "Of course we are only here to avoid a costs sanction and I have told the client it's a waste of time and he shouldn't settle, just find out what the other side's best offer is to see how they really view the case." How do you, as counsel, deal with the situation?
>
> 3. At the opening session you made great play of the fact that your client has attendance notes of critical conversations. In private session your client pulls out his or her original file to show you an invoice missed out of the mediation bundle. Idly flicking through you notice a manuscript note of one of the critical meetings which seems to be very different from the typed note you have relied on. What do you do? Does it matter if it is pre- or post- disclosure in the litigation? The client is adamant the original note should not be disclosed to the other side whilst the mediation is in progress. Would it make any difference if you hadn't relied on attendance notes in your opening?
>
> 4. Your client tells you that he has got some 'dirt' on the other party and wants you to have a private meeting with counsel on the other side and threaten that it will all come out in court/report him to authorities if he doesn't settle. What do you do?
>
> 5. The mediator asks to see your client for a private chat between the two of them (i.e. in your absence? What should you do?
>
> 6. You go to use the telephone in your private caucus room and discover an object attached to it which looks like a bugging device. What do you do?
>
> 7. As you are putting on your coats to leave the mediator suddenly comes in with an increased offer from the other side and presses your

11 I am grateful to a number of professional colleagues who have provided these to me for educational purposes.

client to do a deal there and then. The mediator says that he has tickets to the opera that evening and takes a dim view of counsel who can't see when it is time to tell their client to settle. What do you do?

8. You are going through the draft agreement with your client. He tells you that it is important to make the full and final settlement clause as wide as possible because, quite separate from the current dispute, he owes the other side £90k and if he can slip in a clause which stops them recovering it, that would be all to the good. What do you do?

9. At the last moment your client refuses to sign an agreement which you and he have spent all day negotiating and which you think is an absolute steal. What do you do? Should you behave differently if you know him to have a high conflict personality?

10. On your client's instructions (who is defendant to an action) you give a detailed explanation of why he would not be able to meet any judgment and therefore proceeding to litigation would be a waste of money for the other side. When figures are discussed, your client seems willing to accept an offer that on your instructions (and on the information given to the other side) he should not be able to pay. He then tells you that he has a house in France that could be realised to meet the judgment. He says he forgot to tell you but he does not want this to be communicated to the other side and says in support that the other side must have realised that he could get access to other assets to pay the amount requested. What do you do?

11. You have provided some draft witness statements endorsed on their face as 'privileged, for purposes of mediation only' basis. During the mediation your client receives an irate phone call from one of the witnesses saying she has just been phoned up by the other side who attempted to cross-examine her on her witness statement. What do you do?

12. The other party has made a final global (i.e. inclusive of costs) offer. Your solicitor but not you are on Conditional Fee Agreement (or its latest equivalent) and there is now conflict between your lay and professional clients which needs resolving. What can you/should you do?

Chapter 8
A Note on the Singapore Convention on Mediation 2019

The Singapore Convention on Mediation is a Private International Law agreement which establishes a uniform framework for the effective recognition and enforcement of commercial mediated settlement agreements across borders. It provides a process whereby someone seeking to rely upon a mediated settlement agreement can apply directly to the competent authority of a Party to the Convention to enforce the agreement.

The Convention was negotiated by the United Nations Commission on International Trade Law (UNCITRAL) and came into force on 12 September 2020. It currently has 55 signatories and 9 parties have ratified it.

It was finalised at the fifty-first UNCITRAL Commission session, which came to a close in July 2018. The amended Model Law (the UNCITRAL Model Law on International Commercial Mediation and International Settlement Agreements Resulting from Mediation (2018)) was also adopted at the same session, and the text was then passed to the UN General Assembly which, in December 2018, by consensus, passed a resolution to adopt it, authorised the signing ceremony of the Convention to be held in Singapore on 7 August 2019 after which it would become known as the "Singapore Convention on Mediation".

In the fullness of time the number of signatories and ratifying states will increase, but important original signatories included the world's two largest economies – the United States and China – as well as three of the four largest economies in Asia – China, India and South Korea – signed the Convention on the day it opened for signature. Another 24 countries attended the signing ceremony in Singapore to show their support for the Convention. Japan became a signatory in October 2023 and ratified in April 2024.

On 25 February 2020, Singapore and Fiji became the first two countries to deposit their respective instruments of ratification of the Convention at the United Nations Headquarters in New York. With the third instrument of ratification deposited by Qatar on 12 March 2020, the Convention entered into force on 12 September 2020.

Between February and April, 2022 the UK Government consulted on whether to become a signatory. In the 'consultation description' the following information was given which you may find remarkable:

"The mediation sector in the UK was estimated to be worth £17.5 billion in 2020, and it is estimated that mediation can save businesses around £4.6 billion per year in management time, relationships, productivity and legal fees."

Given that the legal services sector provides a gross value added figure to the UK economy of approximately £60 billion[1] that is a very high proportion of legal spend should the figures be capable of correlation. It also does not appear to reflect the number of cases passing from litigation to mediation, which generally plateaux for a couple of years before moving upwards.

The United Kingdom became a signatory to the Convention on 3 May, 2023. The most notable absentees of major trading countries are the member states of the European Union.

Why was the Convention necessary?

According to its authors it provides a harmonised framework for the enforcement and invocation of international settlement agreements resulting from mediation. In so doing it is intended to facilitate international trade, promote mediation as an alternative and effective method of resolving trade disputes and meet the problem a pre-existing lack of international mediated settlement agreements reached by parties becoming binding and enforceable under a simplified and streamlined procedure. It will thereby help to strengthen access to justice and the rule of law, and promote certainty and stability in the field of international commercial mediation. This contributes to the development of a mature, rules-based global commercial system within the remit of UNCITRAL.

What is its importance to practitioners?

The Convention is a short instrument of only 16 articles, the heart of which is perhaps contained in only three of them. Article 2(3) contains a definition of 'mediation' which incorporates for its purpose the word 'conciliation'

"Mediation" means a process, irrespective of the expression used or the basis upon which the process is carried out, whereby parties attempt to reach an amicable settlement of their dispute, with the assistance of a third person or persons ('the mediator') lacking the authority to impose a solution upon the parties to the dispute.'

The explanatory notes[2] say that 'mediation is a process for discussing and resolving disputes. It is known for improving the efficiency of dispute resolution and offering flexibility to the parties. It is a party-driven process whereby the mediator's role is not to adjudicate, but rather to facilitate discussions between disputing parties to arrive at a mutually acceptable solution. The nature of the process promotes the preservation of relationships between the parties. The mediation process is also flexible, confidential, and in many instances, more cost and time efficient than other dispute resolution processes such as litigation and arbitration. For States, the process can help relieve pressure on the state court system.'

---

1 Law Society Research department and KPMG commissioned report Aug 2019. *N.B.* this was before Covid, based on 2018 figures.

2 https://www.singaporeconvention.org/convention/text The Singapore Convention on Mediation website is managed by the Singapore International Dispute Resolution Academy (SIDRA) in co-operation with the Ministry of Law, Singapore.

The key principles on which the Convention operates are as follows, but the complete text is annexed to this note.

- Only international commercial settlement agreements resulting from mediation can be enforced under the SCM.

The mediation settlement agreement must be international in character (Art 1(1) SCM)

The mediation settlement agreement must be commercial. This excludes disputes arising from transactions by consumers for personal, family, or household purposes, or relating to family, inheritance, or employment law (Art 1(2) SCM)

- The Convention does not apply to settlement agreements that are enforceable as a judgement or arbitral award (Art 1(3)(b) SCM).

A settlement agreement has a dual function under the SCM.

Settlement agreements can be directly enforced in the competent authority of a Party state, in accordance with its rules of procedure and under the conditions laid down in the Convention. (Art 3(1) SCM)

Where a dispute arises relating to a matter which has already been resolved by the settlement agreement, the agreement can be invoked to prove that the matter has been resolved. (Art 3(2) SCM)

The competent authority of a Party state to the SCM may refuse to grant relief on the grounds laid down in the SCM, including:

- If a party to the settlement agreement was under incapacity. (Art 5(1)(a) SCM)

If the settlement agreement is not binding, null and void, inoperative or incapable of being performed under the law to which it is subjected, or has been subsequently modified. (Art 5(1)(b) SCM)

If there was a serious breach by the mediator in terms of applicable mediator standards (Art 5(1)(e) SCM), or failure to disclose circumstances that raise doubts as to mediator impartiality or independence (Art 5(1)(f) SCM), without which the party would not have entered into the agreement.

If granting relief would be contrary to the public policy of the Party state. (Art 5(2)(a) SCM)

- Lastly, Parties to the SCM have been given the option to make the following reservations when signing the SCM:

To qualify that the Convention would not be applicable to settlement agreements to which its government or other public entities are a party. (Art 8(1)(a) SCM)

To adopt an opt-in approach which provides that the Convention only applies to the extent that the disputing parties agree to its application. (Art 8(1)(b) SCM)

Practitioners should note that the Convention recognises important carve outs dealing with domestic jurisdictions that have their own procedure to enforce cross-border mediated settlements. It is also interesting to see that improper conduct by the mediator can negate the enforceability of settlement agreements, and this may be reflected in the cultural considerations already discussed in Chapter 6.[3]

Referring to the travaux préparatoires of the Convention can provide useful insights into the drafter's intentions when the Convention text was being prepared. These are referenced on the Convention website[4] and cover the official preparatory documents from the UNCITRAL Working Group II dealing with negotiations on the final treaty text, dating back to 2015.

---

3 See pp79.

4 https://www.singaporeconvention.org/travaux/about

Appendices

Appendix 1

United Nations Convention on International Settlement Agreements Resulting from Mediation

UNITED NATIONS

New York, 2019

Contents

Resolution adopted by the General Assembly on 20 December 2018

[on the report of the Sixth Committee (A/73/496)]

73/198. United Nations Convention on International Settlement Agreements Resulting from Mediation

The General Assembly,

Recalling its resolution 2205 (XXI) of 17 December 1966, by which it established the United Nations Commission on International Trade Law with a mandate to further the progressive harmonization and unification of the law of international trade and in that respect to bear in mind the interests of all peoples, in particular those of developing countries, in the extensive development of international trade,

Recalling also its resolution 57/18 of 19 November 2002, in which it noted the adoption by the Commission of the Model Law on International Commercial Conciliation[1] and expressed the conviction that the Model Law, together with the Conciliation Rules of the Commission[2] recommended in its resolution 35/52 of 4 December 1980, contributes significantly to the establishment of a harmonized legal framework for the fair and efficient settlement of disputes arising in international commercial relations,

Recognizing the value of mediation as a method of amicably settling disputes arising in the context of international commercial relations,

Convinced that the adoption of a convention on international settlement agreements resulting from mediation that is acceptable to States with different legal, social and economic systems would complement the existing legal framework on international mediation and contribute to the development of harmonious international economic relations,

Noting that the decision of the Commission to concurrently prepare a convention on international settlement agreements resulting from mediation and an amendment to the Model Law on International Commercial Conciliation was intended to accommodate the different levels of experience with mediation in different jurisdictions and to provide States with consistent standards on the cross-border enforcement of international settlement agreements resulting from mediation, without creating any expectation that interested States may adopt either instrument,[3]

1 Resolution 57/18, annex.

2 Official Records of the General Assembly, Thirty-fifth Session, Supplement No. 17 (A/35/17), para. 106; see also Yearbook of the United Nations Commission on International Trade Law, vol. XI: 1980, part three, annex II.

3 Official Records of the General Assembly, Seventy-second Session, Supplement No. 17 (A/72/17), paras. 238–239; see also A/CN.9/901, para. 52.

Noting with satisfaction that the preparation of the draft convention was the subject of due deliberation and that the draft convention benefited from consultations with Governments as well as intergovernmental and non-governmental organizations,

Taking note of the decision of the Commission at its fifty-first session to submit the draft convention to the General Assembly for its consideration,[4]

Taking note with satisfaction of the draft convention approved by the Commission,[5]

Expressing its appreciation to the Government of Singapore for its offer to host a signing ceremony for the Convention in Singapore,

1. *Commends* the United Nations Commission on International Trade Law for preparing the draft convention on international settlement agreements resulting from mediation;

2. *Adopts* the United Nations Convention on International Settlement Agreements Resulting from Mediation, contained in the annex to the present resolution;

3. *Authorizes* a ceremony for the opening for signature of the Convention to be held in Singapore on 7 August 2019, and recommends that the Convention be known as the "Singapore Convention on Mediation";

4. *Calls upon* those Governments and regional economic integration organizations that wish to strengthen the legal framework on international dispute settlement to consider becoming a party to the Convention.

62nd plenary meeting

20 December 2018

4 Official Records of the General Assembly, Seventy-third Session, Supplement No. 17 (A/73/17), para. 49.

5 Ibid., annex I.

United Nations Convention on International Settlement Agreements Resulting from Mediation

Preamble

The Parties to this Convention,

Recognizing the value for international trade of mediation as a method for settling commercial disputes in which the parties in dispute request a third person or persons to assist them in their attempt to settle the dispute amicably,

Noting that mediation is increasingly used in international and domestic commercial practice as an alternative to litigation,

Considering that the use of mediation results in significant benefits, such as reducing the instances where a dispute leads to the termination of a commercial relationship, facilitating the administration of international transactions by commercial parties and producing savings in the administration of justice by States,

Convinced that the establishment of a framework for international settlement agreements resulting from mediation that is acceptable to States with different legal, social and economic systems would contribute to the development of harmonious international economic relations,

Have agreed as follows:

Article 1. Scope of application

1. This Convention applies to an agreement resulting from mediation and concluded in writing by parties to resolve a commercial dispute ("settlement agreement") which, at the time of its conclusion, is international in that:

(a) At least two parties to the settlement agreement have their places of business in different States; or

(b) The State in which the parties to the settlement agreement have their places of business is different from either:

(i) The State in which a substantial part of the obligations under the settlement agreement is performed; or

(ii) The State with which the subject matter of the settlement agreement is most closely connected.

2. This Convention does not apply to settlement agreements:

(a) Concluded to resolve a dispute arising from transactions engaged in by one of the parties (a consumer) for personal, family or household purposes;

(b) Relating to family, inheritance or employment law.

3. This Convention does not apply to:

(a) Settlement agreements:

(i) That have been approved by a court or concluded in the course of proceedings before a court; and

(ii) That are enforceable as a judgment in the State of that court;

(b) Settlement agreements that have been recorded and are enforceable as an arbitral award.

Article 2. Definitions

1. For the purposes of article 1, paragraph 1:

(a) If a party has more than one place of business, the relevant place of business is that which has the closest relationship to the dispute resolved by the settlement agreement, having regard to the circumstances known to, or contemplated by, the parties at the time of the conclusion of the settlement agreement;

(b) If a party does not have a place of business, reference is to be made to the party's habitual residence.

2. A settlement agreement is "in writing" if its content is recorded in any form. The requirement that a settlement agreement be in writing is met by an electronic communication if the information contained therein is accessible so as to be useable for subsequent reference.

3. "Mediation" means a process, irrespective of the expression used or the basis upon which the process is carried out, whereby parties attempt to reach an amicable settlement of their dispute with the assistance of a third person or persons ("the mediator") lacking the authority to impose a solution upon the parties to the dispute.

Article 3. General principles

1. Each Party to the Convention shall enforce a settlement agreement in accordance with its rules of procedure and under the conditions laid down in this Convention.

2. If a dispute arises concerning a matter that a party claims was already resolved by a settlement agreement, a Party to the Convention shall allow the party to invoke the settlement agreement in accordance with its rules of procedure and under the conditions laid down in this Convention, in order to prove that the matter has already been resolved.

Article 4. Requirements for reliance on settlement agreements

1. A party relying on a settlement agreement under this Convention shall supply to the competent authority of the Party to the Convention where relief is sought:

(a) The settlement agreement signed by the parties;

(b) Evidence that the settlement agreement resulted from mediation, such as:

(i) The mediator's signature on the settlement agreement;

(ii) A document signed by the mediator indicating that the mediation was carried out;

(iii) An attestation by the institution that administered the mediation; or

(iv) In the absence of (i), (ii) or (iii), any other evidence acceptable to the competent authority.

2. The requirement that a settlement agreement shall be signed by the parties or, where applicable, the mediator is met in relation to an electronic communication if:

(a) A method is used to identify the parties or the mediator and to indicate the parties' or mediator's intention in respect of the information contained in the electronic communication; and

(b) The method used is either:

(i) As reliable as appropriate for the purpose for which the electronic communication was generated or communicated, in the light of all the circumstances, including any relevant agreement; or

(ii) Proven in fact to have fulfilled the functions described in subparagraph (a) above, by itself or together with further evidence.

3. If the settlement agreement is not in an official language of the Party to the Convention where relief is sought, the competent authority may request a translation thereof into such language.

4. The competent authority may require any necessary document in order to verify that the requirements of the Convention have been complied with.

5. When considering the request for relief, the competent authority shall act expeditiously.

Article 5. Grounds for refusing to grant relief

1. The competent authority of the Party to the Convention where relief is sought under article 4 may refuse to grant relief at the request of the party against whom the relief is sought only if that party furnishes to the competent authority proof that:

(a) A party to the settlement agreement was under some incapacity;

(b) The settlement agreement sought to be relied upon:

(i) Is null and void, inoperative or incapable of being performed under the law to which the parties have validly subjected it or, failing any indication thereon, under the law deemed applicable by the competent authority of the Party to the Convention where relief is sought under article 4;

(ii) Is not binding, or is not final, according to its terms; or

(iii) Has been subsequently modified;

(c) The obligations in the settlement agreement:

(i) Have been performed; or

(ii) Are not clear or comprehensible;

(d) Granting relief would be contrary to the terms of the settlement agreement;

(e) There was a serious breach by the mediator of standards applicable to the mediator or the mediation without which breach that party would not have entered into the settlement agreement; or

(f) There was a failure by the mediator to disclose to the parties circumstances that raise justifiable doubts as to the mediator's impartiality or independence and such failure to disclose had a material impact or undue influence on a party without which failure that party would not have entered into the settlement agreement.

2. The competent authority of the Party to the Convention where relief is sought under article 4 may also refuse to grant relief if it finds that:

(a) Granting relief would be contrary to the public policy of that Party; or

(b) The subject matter of the dispute is not capable of settlement by mediation under the law of that Party.

Article 6. Parallel applications or claims

If an application or a claim relating to a settlement agreement has been made to a court, an arbitral tribunal or any other competent authority which may affect the relief being sought under article 4, the competent authority of the Party to the Convention where such relief is sought may, if it considers it proper, adjourn the decision and may also, on the request of a party, order the other party to give suitable security.

Article 7. Other laws or treaties

This Convention shall not deprive any interested party of any right it may have to avail itself of a settlement agreement in the manner and to the extent allowed by the law or the treaties of the Party to the Convention where such settlement agreement is sought to be relied upon.

Article 8. Reservations

1. A Party to the Convention may declare that:

(a) It shall not apply this Convention to settlement agreements to which it is a party, or to which any governmental agencies or any person acting on behalf of a governmental agency is a party, to the extent specified in the declaration;

(b) It shall apply this Convention only to the extent that the parties to the settlement agreement have agreed to the application of the Convention.

2. No reservations are permitted except those expressly authorized in this article.

3. Reservations may be made by a Party to the Convention at any time. Reservations made at the time of signature shall be subject to confirmation upon ratification, acceptance or approval. Such reservations shall take effect simultaneously with the entry into force of this Convention in respect of the Party to the Convention concerned. Reservations made at the time of ratification, acceptance or approval of this Convention or accession thereto, or at the time of making a declaration under article 13 shall take effect simultaneously with the entry into force of this Convention in respect of the Party to the Convention concerned. Reservations deposited after the entry into force of the Convention for that Party to the Convention shall take effect six months after the date of the deposit.

4. Reservations and their confirmations shall be deposited with the depositary.

5. Any Party to the Convention that makes a reservation under this Convention may withdraw it at any time. Such withdrawals are to be deposited with the depositary, and shall take effect six months after deposit.

Article 9. Effect on settlement agreements

The Convention and any reservation or withdrawal thereof shall apply only to settlement agreements concluded after the date when the Convention, reservation or withdrawal thereof enters into force for the Party to the Convention concerned.

Article 10. Depositary

The Secretary-General of the United Nations is hereby designated as the depositary of this Convention.

Article 11. Signature, ratification, acceptance, approval, accession

1. This Convention is open for signature by all States in Singapore, on 7 August 2019, and thereafter at United Nations Headquarters in New York.

2. This Convention is subject to ratification, acceptance or approval by the signatories.

3. This Convention is open for accession by all States that are not signatories as from the date it is open for signature.

4. Instruments of ratification, acceptance, approval or accession are to be deposited with the depositary.

Article 12. Participation by regional economic integration organizations

1. A regional economic integration organization that is constitut d by sovereign States and has competence over certain matters governed by this Convention may similarly sign, ratify, accept, approve or accede to this Convention. The regional economic integration organization shall in that case have the rights and obligations of a Party to the Convention, to the extent that that organization has competence over matters governed by this Convention. Where the number of Parties to the Convention is relevant in this Convention, the regional economic integration organization shall not count as a Party to the Convention in addition to its member States that are Parties to the Convention.

2. The regional economic integration organization shall, at the time of signature, ratification, acceptance, approval or accession, make a declaration to the depositary specifying the matters governed by this Convention in respect of which competence has been transferred to that organization by its member States. The regional economic integration organization shall promptly notify the depositary of any changes to the distribution of competence, including new transfers of competence, specified in the declaration under this paragraph.

3. Any reference to a "Party to the Convention", "Parties to the Convention", a "State" or "States" in this Convention applies equally to a regional economic integration organization where the context so requires.

4. This Convention shall not prevail over conflicting rules of a regional economic integration organization, whether such rules were adopted or entered into force before or after this Convention: (a) if, under article 4, relief is sought in a State that is member of such an organization and all the States relevant under article 1, paragraph 1, are members of such an organization; or (b) as concerns the recognition or enforcement of judgments between member States of such an organization.

Article 13. Non-unified legal systems

1. If a Party to the Convention has two or more territorial units in which different systems of law are applicable in relation to the matters dealt with in this Convention, it may, at the time of signature, ratification, acceptance, approval or accession, declare that this Convention is to extend to all its territorial units or only to one or more of them, and may amend its declaration by submitting another declaration at any time.

2. These declarations are to be notified to the depositary and are to state expressly the territorial units to which the Convention extends.

3. If a Party to the Convention has two or more territorial units in which different systems of law are applicable in relation to the matters dealt with in this Convention:

(a) Any reference to the law or rule of procedure of a State shall be construed as referring, where appropriate, to the law or rule of procedure in force in the relevant territorial unit;

(b) Any reference to the place of business in a State shall be construed as referring, where appropriate, to the place of business in the relevant territorial unit;

(c) Any reference to the competent authority of the State shall be construed as referring, where appropriate, to the competent authority in the relevant territorial unit.

4. If a Party to the Convention makes no declaration under paragraph 1 of this article, the Convention is to extend to all territorial units of that State.

Article 14. Entry into force

1. This Convention shall enter into force six months after deposit of the third instrument of ratification, acceptance, approval or accession.

2. When a State ratifies, accepts, approves or accedes to this Convention after the deposit of the third instrument of ratification, acceptance, approval or accession, this Convention shall enter into force in respect of that State six months after the date of the deposit of its instrument of ratification, acceptance, approval or accession. The Convention shall enter into force for a territorial unit to which this Convention has been extended in accordance with article 13 six months after the notification of the declaration referred to in that article.

Article 15. Amendment

1. Any Party to the Convention may propose an amendment to the present Convention by submitting it to the Secretary-General of the United Nations. The Secretary-General shall thereupon communicate the proposed amendment to the Parties to the Convention with a request that they indicate whether they favour a conference of Parties to the Convention for the purpose of considering and voting upon the proposal. In the event that within four months from the date of such communication at least one third of the Parties to the Convention favour such a conference, the Secretary-General shall convene the conference under the auspices of the United Nations.

2. The conference of Parties to the Convention shall make every effort to achieve consensus on each amendment. If all efforts at consensus are exhausted and no consensus is reached, the amendment shall, as a last resort, require for its adoption a two-thirds majority vote of the Parties to the Convention present and voting at the conference.

3. An adopted amendment shall be submitted by the depositary to all the Parties to the Convention for ratification, acceptance or approval.

4. An adopted amendment shall enter into force six months after the date of deposit of the third instrument of ratification, acceptance or approval. When an amendment enters into force, it shall be binding on those Parties to the Convention that have expressed consent to be bound by it.

5. When a Party to the Convention ratifies, accepts or approves an amendment following the deposit of the third instrument of ratification, acceptance or approval, the amendment shall enter into force in respect of that Party to the Convention six months after the date of the deposit of its instrument of ratification, acceptance or approval.

Article 16. Denunciations

1. A Party to the Convention may denounce this Convention by a formal notification in writing addressed to the depositary. The denunciation may be limited to certain territorial units of a nonunified legal system to which this Convention applies.

2. The denunciation shall take effect 12 months after the notification is received by the depositary. Where a longer period for the denunciation to take effect is specified in the notification, the denunciation shall take effect upon the expiration of such longer period after the notification is received by the depositary. The Convention shall continue to apply to settlement agreements concluded before the denunciation takes effect.

DONE in a single original, of which the Arabic, Chinese, English, French, Russian and Spanish texts are equally authentic.

Appendix 2
A Note on COVID 19

Mediation, Facilitation, Contracting and Crisis Management

For more than two years commercial enterprise all over the world came to face the kind of challenge rarely seen outside wartime, with transport, oil and gas, supply chains, logistics, property, retail and hospitality suffering the wholesale suspension of trading activities, and either lockdown or the restriction of personal social liberties affecting millions of people across the world. The logistics industry recovered reasonably strongly and food suppliers are now doing well, albeit they have their own concerns with the impact of regional wars, piracy at sea, and the impact of Brexit and a faltering Chinese economy. However, the number of liquidations and personal insolvency, mass unemployment and the scale of governmental intervention will not in combination have been seen before by anyone now living, particularly in the Western democracies where citizens have a right to question the decision-making of government.

The enormity of the potential problems which have faced most of us over the last three years pose questions in every sector concerning whether the conduct of business would ever return to normal, or whether profound change would occur in the way in which we engage with each other? As business moved online, and home working became and remains a matter of course, and as our city centres emptied, what will the future of commerce look like? At the time of writing large corporations and civil services around the world are still struggling to get their workforces to return to the office.

In the short term, lawyers will be considering the parameters of existing contracts: can liability for ongoing contractual performance be enforced, or will such liability be suspended by operation of *force majeure*? Has the contract been frustrated? Will the parties take a commercially realistic view and re-negotiate the contract? Can they be forced to do so? What mechanisms inside or outside the contract would permit them so to do? Are losses covered by business interruption insurance? What happens if the insurer avoids the policy? What flows from a party's insolvency? Or an insurer's insolvency? What will happen to businesses upwards and downwards in the supply chain? Will state aid provide commerce with a safety net? How will the state intervene if it is restricted by the regulation of its economy by supra-national institutions or by international treaty?

In the longer term, how should contracts take in the possibility of further waves of pandemic, or new pandemics occurring? Just before the time of writing Shanghai remained in lockdown and science had not even begun to consider long term mutations of the present virus, irrespective of announcements offering the confidence of new vaccines as a means of returning to normality. How can contracts be designed to accommodate crises with a flexible but realistic response?

These are matters of concern to the whole of commerce, and not confined to the academic theory of the law. Business may require a more enduring strategy based on an innovative approach, and a mechanism to renegotiate contracts or rethink entire relationships using a mediative process to generate previously unseen options. Relying on the legal doctrines of frustration, force majeure and supervening impossibility seems anachronistic.

All around the world it has been demonstrated that courts are poorly equipped – if at all - to provide the kind of responsive and immediate remedies that commerce needs for business to flow in the face of such difficulties. Even if they could support enterprise with the modern approach that is needed, delays have now forced civil justice systems to realise their own deficiencies. There is little point in a claimant obtaining a judgment that cannot be enforced due to the insolvency or impending insolvency of the defendant. The broader, but less common, range of other relief available in equity is equally unsuitable since courts are principally concerned with giving effect to the intention of the parties at the time of entry into the transaction. Courts cannot re-write contracts or supervise renegotiation by the parties; nor can they bring in non-parties or those likely to be affected as a consequence of renegotiation.

But mediators, facilitators and conciliators, with the participation of the parties and their lawyers, can. We should be on the fringes of a golden age for commercial mediation based not merely on the resolution of disputes but helping parties to renegotiate their contractual relationships.

Significantly now, many businesses are being forced to ask simple questions, either can I enforce a particular contractual obligation, or else, do I have to perform/pay?

The lawyer or contracts manager will first see if there is either a force majeure clause in the relevant contract, or something like it. A force majeure clause typically excuses a party seeking to rely on it from performance of a contractual obligation, usually temporarily, following the occurrence of certain events, usually defined as acts, events or circumstances beyond the reasonable control of the party concerned.

If there is a force majeure clause in such a contract it is possible that COVID-19 may be covered, depending on the wording of the clause, which will list examples of the events that fall within its scope. For example, the clause might specifically list "pandemics" or refer to contagions. It may also be covered under an "Act of God" which was defined under English law by Lord Hobhouse in *Transco PLC v Stockport Metropolitan Borough Council,*[1] as an act which, (i) involves no human agency; (ii) is not realistically possible to guard against; (iii) is due exclusively and directly to natural causes; and, (iv) could not have been prevented against with any amount of foresight, plans, and care. Finally, it is also possible that the clause will refer to government

1 [2003] UKHL 61

actions, which would include the wholesale closure of cities within the United Kingdom, and countries within Europe or elsewhere, and any restrictions placed on travel or imports by governments, including quarantine where relevant.

The party seeking to rely on the clause to avoid its obligations will likely have also to show that: (i) its non-performance or default was caused by the force majeure event (and not by, for example, an act or omission within the party's own control); (ii) that the force majeure event has made it legally or physically impossible to perform its obligations; (iii) there were no reasonable steps that one could have taken to avoid or mitigate the event or its consequences. It appears to be trite law that such obligations do not extend to the simple requirement to make payment.

This is, of course, all subject to the express wording of the contractual provision which the parties had the foresight to include on execution. In addition it should be remembered under English law a party cannot rely on the clause unless it is ready, willing and able to perform its contractual duties if the force majeure event had not occurred (*Classic Maritime Inc v Limbungan Makmur SDN BHD & Anor* [2]). The burden of proof is on the party seeking to rely on the force majeure clause, who must prove that the event (in this case COVID-19) falls within the force majeure clause and that non-performance of contractual obligations was due to the event.

On the other hand lawyers acting in correspondence prior to the issue of a claim will recognise that if a party opposite is seeking to rely on a force majeure clause to avoid its contractual obligations and it is unclear whether COVID-19 is covered by the clause, in order to prevent implicit or express waiver of contractual rights, that correspondence should be handled very carefully. If COVID-19 is clearly covered by a force majeure clause, it might be more prudent, more cost effective and more likely to meet the client's immediate needs to consider negotiating with the other party to see if a workable solution can be achieved. Otherwise it may be appropriate to include in dealing with other parties either, in bringing forward assertions, or even as part of a renegotiation, an express reservation that nothing you have said should be taken as a waiver of your client's contractual rights.

If your client is seeking to avoid contractual obligations and there is no force majeure clause in the relevant contract, there may still be a remedy available under the legal doctrine of frustration where performance has become commercially or physically impossible. A parallel American law doctrine of impossibility or frustration of purpose exists although the bar for resisting the original obligation is high since the starting point for a court is to hold parties to their bargain, if possible, and that also remains the starting point for example for an obligation under Sharia: if there is a different way for the parties to perform their contract, even if it is more expensive or more difficult than the original expected method of performance, the Court will seek to enforce that form of performance.

Whether it is open to claim the effects of COVID-19 amount to a frustration event successfully to avoid contractual obligations will be specific to the

2 [2019] EWCA Civ 1102

contract and the facts of each case. If a government has put mandatory restrictions in place as a result of the outbreak/spread/occurrence of COVID-19 that is not due to the fault of either party. If this occurs after the contract has been formed and it makes future performance impossible, illegal or makes it so fundamentally different from that contemplated by the parties at the time of the contact, there are reasonable grounds for claiming frustration.

As I have said, if the contractual obligation is merely to make a payment, neither force majeure nor frustration are likely to be of immediate assistance. If you are found in this position, where possible, it is worth taking steps to attempt to mitigate your loss by re-negotiating with the other party as to what is a sensible commercial solution. If there are to be future commercial relations between you, that may be the best solution for you both: don't fight your way out of a problem when it is open to you to trade your way out of it. Both of these approaches are likely to engage mediation as the appropriate mechanism for parties who cannot come to a satisfactory outcome by themselves.

If a party can prove that an event giving rise to frustration has occurred, the contract is automatically discharged and that brings an end to the parties' obligations. There is no option for a party to elect to continue the contract. If one party has paid money to another under a contract before the occurrence of the frustrating event (for example, money paid as an advance in consideration for the future supply of goods or services), it may be possible under English law to recover monies paid (or at least a portion of monies paid) under the contract under the Law Reform (Frustrated Contracts) Act 1943 and elsewhere, possibly by more creative arguments relying on the law of unjust enrichment or restitutionary principles that have substantially developed since the 1943 Act. Again, the creativity of a mediator in helping the parties to generate options not available to the courts is an avenue that business should seek, and advocates have an important role in bringing this opportunity to the attention of their clients.

It is now clear that the spread of COVID-19 will have had an impact on hundreds of thousands of contracts worldwide and is likely to be an ongoing problem stretching into the future. While the practitioner must ensure clients are aware of their contractual rights and obligations, to be able to act quickly, and be careful in dealings had in correspondence with the other party, mediation looks like a very attractive vehicle for those who need to negotiate in a managed process.

That addresses the short-term problem. But what of contracts in an age where the residual impact of a pandemic is a cause of continuing concern?

The starting point will be for all businesses to review their key contracts as soon as possible. Their legal or contracts departments or external lawyers will need to consider:

- What are the parties' obligations under the contract, and when must they be performed? Are the obligations stated sufficiently clearly?

- How does COVID-19 impact on the parties' ability to perform their respective obligations under the contract? What specific practical difficulties does it create?

- Does the contract contain provisions allowing one or both parties to terminate it, or postpone performance? If so, in what circumstances can the parties do so?

- Does the contract explain what the consequences of termination, or delayed performance, would be? What are the financial consequences for the parties, and do they risk being sued for a failure to perform their side of the bargain?

- Is performance of the contract physically or commercially impossible, such that it may have been frustrated?

- Or, can either or both parties rely on coronavirus and its effects as a force majeure event? Is there an express force majeure clause in the agreement? What, in practice, are the consequences of invoking it?

- What would the client ideally like to achieve – ending, suspending or varying the contract – and how important is it to preserve one side's commercial relationship with the other party?

Whilst there may be short-term solutions to this problem, and each contract will need to be considered on its own specific facts, for those engaged in a mediation-based renegotiation the mediation advocate will need to work out what each party's legal position is likely to be. This will inform your negotiations with the other party in seeking new contractual arrangements.

In addition the disruption caused by coronavirus has inevitably led organisations and individuals to review their insurance policies to see whether the risks and potential losses arising from the virus and from the government's reaction to it are covered, particularly the indemnity offered either under an all risks policy, or one dedicated to business interruption insurance. In September, 2020 the United Kingdom's insurance regulator successfully brought a claim in the English High Court as at test case on liability against eight insurers in respect of COVID-19 Business Interruption insurance. *The Financial Conduct Authority v Arch and Others*[3] considered 21 lead sample wording across 60 insurers in respect of 370,000 policy holders, most of which were SMEs. Following expedited proceedings, the judgment of the UK Supreme Court[4] in broadly dismissing the insurers' appeals, brought highly-anticipated guidance on the proper operation of cover under certain non-damage business interruption insurance extensions.

Most of us are likely to need specialist advice, perhaps from a chartered loss adjuster, to understand whether and how insurance policies may help deal with the current situation and as it evolves in the future. An initial consideration may be to understand what "risks" are covered, and what are

3 [2020] EWHC 2448 (Comm)

4 [2021] UKSC 1

excluded. Even though standard commercial insurance policies usually cover a wide range of risks under an 'all risks policy', they are unlikely to cover specialised or unlikely risks, such as the effects of coronavirus, and newer policies may exclude coronavirus as a "pre-existing circumstance". The *Arch* case provided a welcome respite to many businesses that were facing an uphill battle to obtain indemnities they were due.

Even if your policy does include notifiable disease as a risk, check to see that it does not fall into any of the exclusions (for example, a mutant variation of atypical pneumonia or SARS) and that you are still covered. As every policy needs to be considered on its own terms and the specific facts relevant to the possible claim, advising upon and understanding rights may not be easy, and may itself give rise to dispute.

The scope and nature of business interruption cover should extend to cover for the loss of directors or key personnel, and trustees, of the corporations or institutions you act for, and you will need to navigate the risks they may face both as organisations and their officers personally.

In more general terms the way of the future may lie in facilitation. In 2022 the London Academy of Arbitration and Mediation (LCAM) published a Protocol for Facilitated Contract Renegotiation which is the first institutionalised method of addressing some of these issues. Such an approach removes the focus on disputes and is proactive in seeking to preserve the commercial relationship of parties to a contract before a potential dispute emerges or crystallises. It may be less clunky than mediation, and certainly less lawyer driven. It will be interesting to see how this concept develops over time, and we may well see the growth of this hybrid model being offered by other mediation service providers.

May, 2023

Index